BASIC ANTHROPOLOGY UNITS

GENERAL EDITORS
George and Louise Spindler
STANFORD UNIVERSITY

SOCIOCULTURAL THEORY IN ANTHROPOLOGY
A Short History

MERWYN S. GARBARINO
University of Illinois at Chicago Circle

Sociocultural Theory in Anthropology
A Short History

HOLT, RINEHART AND WINSTON
New York Chicago San Francisco Atlanta
Dallas Montreal Toronto London Sydney

Library of Congress Cataloging in Publication Data

Garbarino, Merwyn S.
Sociocultural theory in anthropology.

(Basic anthropology units)
Bibliography: p. 105
Includes index.
1. Ethnology—History.   2. Ethnology—Philoso-
phy.   I. Title.
GN308.G37   301.2'01   76–46509
ISBN: 0–03–013021–2

Foreword

THE BASIC ANTHROPOLOGY UNITS

Basic Anthropology Units are designed to introduce students to essential topics in the contemporary study of man. In combination they have greater depth and scope than any single textbook. They may also be assigned selectively to cover topics relevant to the particular profile of a given course, or they may be utilized separately as authoritative guides to significant aspects of anthropology.

This series was planned over a period of several years by a number of anthropologists, some of whom are authors of the separate Basic Units. The completed series will include units representing all the basic sectors of contemporary anthropology, including archaeology, biological anthropology, and linguistics, as well as the various subfields of social and cultural anthropology.

THE AUTHOR

Merwyn Stephens Garbarino received her Ph.D. in anthropology from Northwestern University and is associate professor of anthropology at the University of Illinois at Chicago Circle where she has been teaching since 1966. After fieldwork among the Mikasuki-speaking Seminole Indians of south Florida, Dr. Garbarino did fieldwork on reservations in the northern plains and the upper Great Lakes. More recently she has done research on Indian urbanization in Chicago. Her theoretical interests include epistemology, the history of ethnology, and the interpretation of anthropological data and concepts for those who are not majors in anthropology. Dr. Garbarino is author of *Big Cypress: A Changing Seminole Community* and *Native American Heritage,* and co-author of *People and Cultures,* a textbook for junior high school social science courses.

THIS UNIT

There is no single variety of resource needed more in the teaching of introductory and intermediate level anthropology courses than a statement, in brief compass, of the major developments in anthropological theory rendered in an historical perspective. This unit is that kind of resource.

Without the kind of orientation this book provides, students ordinarily perceive anthropology as a discipline springing full-blown (with its contemporary characteristics, many of them quite temporary and situational) from the brow of their instructor and from the pages of their texts. Anthropology seems isolated from the history of Western thought to many students. It is rarely taught in high schools and is rarely given anything resembling adequate treatment by historians of Western intellectual development. Students enter the introductory course with caricatures of anthropology and anthropologists in their minds that are still, woefully, images of anthropology created in mass media and perpetuated by folk culture.

This Basic Unit puts contemporary anthropology in perspective. It shows that it, anthropology, has roots in time, and that far from being a marginal interest, it has been for some time a major concern of Western man—emerging with the experience of the West, the growth and consolidation of empires, and the colonial enterprise. With this perspective students can also understand that anthropology is still a part of its sociocultural context. The disintegration of the nineteenth century form of colonialism and the self-assertiveness of the former colonial peoples provide a new context for anthropological research and theory.

Dr. Garbarino has adopted the strategy of presentation that students find most logical and has put theory in historical perspective. *She avoids writing a theory of anthropological theory* and maintains the ability to ascribe an historical documentation to it. Of course, the selective process involved in this documentation is a kind of interpretation, or even *theory of theories,* but distortion has been minimized. The validity of this enterprise cannot be determined in the same way a scientific generalization can be. Rather, it can be estimated by careful scrutiny of others who have immersed themselves in the same kinds of materials and have had approximately the same training in interpretation. This has been done. No Basic Unit in this series has been subjected to more thorough criticism by knowledgeable colleagues than this one.

To be sure, no professional anthropologist is going to be satisfied with the treatment accorded his or her area of specialization. Nearly everyone will find that most other areas are as fairly represented as they can be in a small book. Most knowledgeable readers will be very pleased with the overall coverage of the book, and will realize how much distillation of sources has taken place in order to produce such a succinct statement as this. Students will not become specialists overnight, but the quality of information and statement will assuredly enhance prior perspectives and will lead most to an appreciation of the broad coverage of ideas and history in a book so easy to read and so comparatively brief. This Basic Unit has been classroom tested and is the outgrowth of classroom experience.

Dr. Garbarino's *Sociocultural Theory in Anthropology: A Short History,* in our opinion as teachers of introductory anthropology for more than twenty-five years, will prove to be an indispensable companion to whatever combination of texts one elects to use in the introductory course in social or cultural anthropology. It will also prove useful to junior and senior year students who may want to learn what they *should* have learned in the introductory course, but did not. And many graduate students and professionals will find this Basic Unit very handy for a brush-up on theory.

George and Louise Spindler
General Editors
STANFORD, CALIF.

Preface

This book is a survey of the history of sociocultural theory for introductory anthropology classes. It is intended as an organizing framework, not as a substitute for study of original works or as a replacement of a professor's own interpretations. I have tried to present all theoretical viewpoints fairly, concisely, and simply, and I have not attempted to advance my own theoretical position. Any work so brief must depend upon a high degree of generalization. Details will come only from intensive study of the theorists themselves.

I have briefly incorporated influences from other disciplines and indicated some of the social, economic, and political factors of the periods in which the theories developed, sketching the general historical backgrounds in a paragraph or two and hitting only upon events and attitudes that were especially significant for the development of behavioral science. A paragraph or so cannot possibly explain *all* the events that occur in a full historical picture for a year, let alone a century, but it can offer some appropriate information and I believe that even such a superficial characterization of pertinent history will help fill whatever gaps may exist in students' historical knowledge. In the restricted space allotted, I have made no attempt to cover substantive works by people cited or to include the many fine anthropologists who more or less followed another's theoretical position.

The structure of this book has emerged from my experiences of teaching theory in introductory classes. I have observed that students entering universities and colleges today have little, if any, background in the intellectual history of European thought. References to social philosophy, the Age of Reason, the Enlightenment, and so on strike no responsive chord. This book relates social thought of the past to the present and helps fill this intellectual void. The importance of the book lies in its conciseness. I have wanted for years to possess a digest of theoretical development that would provide an accessible, easy-to-use source of information—one that placed the major figures in our discipline in a chronological framework which showed their relationships to one another. I finally decided to write such a *guide* myself.

I use the word *guide* judiciously: this book is meant to be just that, a sort of map of theoretical positions. Seeing the scholars of our discipline in the historical and intellectual environment of their times makes their theories more memorable as well as more understandable. I am convinced of it. To make the guide brief is to enhance its value as a supplement—or complement—to the original works. Consequently, this history is an abridgement that will ease the chores of preparing for exams, writing papers, reading, and doing research. It will, in addition, save much valuable time in locating pertinent information and references.

Readers may raise objections that many specialties are omitted from the contemporary picture. This is deliberate because while they may be new in practice or subject matter, most current interests fall within one or another of the older theoretical positions—for example, medical anthropology can be pursued from functional, structural, ecological, or cognitive orientations. Though some may disagree, I do not consider such topics as political anthropology, medical anthropology, applied anthropology, urban anthropology, and so on to be theoretical innovations but rather substantive expansion.

Merwyn S. Garbarino

Contents

SOCIOCULTURAL THEORY IN ANTHROPOLOGY
A Short History

The Nature of Anthropology and Sources of Theory

INTRODUCTION

Contemporary Western philosophy—by which we mean the philosophical traditions of Europeans wherever they have settled throughout the world—has its roots in intellectual legacies from earlier times, and anthropology, a part of Western philosophy like other social sciences, is a mosaic of many pieces developing through time. To understand its present form we need to know the materials from which it grew; we need to see how knowledge and ideas developed as people questioned and tested accepted beliefs and traditions. That is the reason for the chronological approach of this book.

Written for students in introductory college courses, this is a survey of general behavioral theory from the standpoint of sociocultural[1] anthropology. It does not deal with specific biological, archaeological, kinship, or linguistic theories except in so far as they have contributed to general ethnological development. Those who might wish to pursue the subject in greater depth should turn to the bibliography which suggests more extensive, detailed, and advanced histories of theory, and collections of readings and other works by authors cited. Another source of original articles is the Bobbs-Merrill reprint series.

Anthropologists have accumulated an immense collection of information—so immense as to be unwieldy. This short history will help organize that information and make it more meaningful and useful. It is also hoped that this book will make the information interesting as students of anthropology look down that long road to the past and see how present notions in the discipline developed. The historical perspective may sober us when we realize how little we have advanced. On the other hand, that perspective teaches that we have made important strides in some areas. And it is, furthermore, interesting to gain glimpses into the lives and thought processes of our "ancestors." The brevity of this book offers the additional advantage of speed in locating vital information about the scholars and their theories,

---

[1] We use the term "sociocultural" to indicate the interrelatedness of human culture and human society. That is, humans are social beings, organized in groups with distinctive cultural (learned) characteristics, histories, and responses to their environments. "Sociocultural" is thus a kind of umbrella term covering interactions and processes of many sorts whereas either single term is less inclusive.

and it provides a useful supplement to the original works for students newly introduced to anthropology.

Since the book has been written for students in American universities, it follows the accepted American usage of terms, unless otherwise indicated. I suggest that as original theoretical works are read, students use this book as a kind of outline to keep the various theorists, their periods, and their "schools" in order.

THE NATURE OF ANTHROPOLOGY

Anthropology is, as the Greek origin of the word implies, the study of man— human beings. But since all the social or behavioral sciences study humans in one way or another, one may legitimately ask just what it is that distinguishes anthropology from sociology, social psychology, biology, or any other social discipline. It is primarily the breadth of coverage that makes anthropology different. Political science studies people in decision-making and power relationships; economics studies production, distribution, and consumption of goods and services; psychology focuses on individual behavior within a particular cultural matrix, and so on. Anthropology combines all these categories and interests and includes many more. It is a comprehensive study of man the animal and man the social being through time and space. Thus, anthropology has been called the *holistic social science.*

In American universities, the discipline is usually subdivided into three categories: physical or biological anthropology, archaeology or prehistory, and sociocultural anthropology. Undergraduates majoring in anthropology take courses in all subareas, but specialization begins in graduate school, and few, if any, professionals have command of the entire discipline. (Since this is written for American audiences, differences in European approaches will be discussed as they come up in the text.)

Subdivisions of Anthropology

Physical anthropology includes the study and interpretation of fossil primate remains, research on living nonhuman primates, population genetics, and the evolution of *Homo sapiens* as a species. Some physical anthropologists do fieldwork searching for remains of ancestral human populations; others study nonhuman primate life in the wild—ethology—to learn more about the social organization and behavior of those creatures biologically closest to humans; others spend most of their research time in laboratories. But it is all part of anthropology.

Archaeologists work from material remains of past societies to reconstruct extinct cultures and to study the processes of culture change. Archaeologists and physical anthropologists add time dimension to anthropology; a dimension largely lacking in other behavioral sciences.

Sociocultural anthropology is the study of human cultures or lifeways, and it is further broken down into *ethnography* and *ethnology.* The description of societies around the world is the domain of ethnography. It is the ethnographer who records the cultures of the various peoples, and usually publishes findings in a book or monograph called an ethnography. Two characteristics set anthropology apart from sociology: the cross-cultural coverage and the fieldwork technique of the ethnographer. The ethnographer in the field tries to participate in the culture of the host society as he observes the behavior, a methodology that is known as participant-observation. That is not to say that ethnographers "go native," but it does indicate an important precept of anthropology: *One cannot truly understand others by observation alone.* Consequently, sociocultural anthropologists have thought it important to immerse themselves in another way of life as active participants. Needless to say, such participants never really become a part of the "other society," or free themselves from their own enculturative experience, but they do gain insight and impressions impossible to achieve from mere observation or interviewing.

Traditionally, the subjects of ethnographic research were people from non-Western and nonindustrialized societies. In fact, at one time, cultural anthropology was considered the study of "native peoples." *Those people* have been called by a number of different terms: primitive, tribal, nonliterate, simple, nonindustrial; terms that have sometimes appeared insulting or degrading, though such was not intended. Since the Second World War, all cultures, including American urban and industrial European, have come within the field of ethnography, and complex societies have become a major target of anthropological research.

The second component of cultural anthropology is ethnology, which consists of theory building about human behavior and the interrelation between behavior and culture. (In Britain, however, ethnology usually refers to the history of people without written records.) Over the years, interaction among the subareas of anthropology and the other sciences and constant revision of information have resulted in increased knowledge about the ways of human beings. As in other disciplines, theories in anthropology have gone through cycles of popularity. Sometimes theories have been abandoned as untenable; some have survived, while many others have been revived and modernized on the basis of new or better data.

Linguistics is sometimes classified as a separate category, but it is often included as a subdivision of cultural anthropology. In the past, when almost all ethnographers described nonliterate peoples, they had to record languages never before put in written form. Consequently, the study of unwritten languages came to be a logical and integral part of anthropology. (Classical and historical linguists are most frequently not classified as anthropologists.) Today, in addition to purely linguistic issues, anthropological linguists study such topics as the interrelatedness of language and other aspects of culture, and questions of cognition cross-culturally.

The discipline of anthropology is not only comprehensive as sketched above, but it is also importantly comparative. Anthropologists, as a group, have not been content to confine their studies to a few societies; they have sought the full range of human behavior. The cross-cultural variation in behavior recorded by anthropologists has provided information about human alternatives, and given the perspective that allows one to take a look at his own society, ways, and values, in a new light. Such comparative study includes variation through time—culture change—as well as the cross-cultural view that results from ethnographic studies.

The field of anthropology seems like a "very mixed bag" to many. However, anthropologists themselves cherish the combination and grand sweep of the discipline and vigorously oppose any attempt to narrow the field. The discipline achieves integration through its major concept, *culture*. Culture has been variously defined, and in succeeding pages, some of the definitions will be presented. At the moment, suffice it to say that culture is learned behavior and the products of that behavior as opposed to instinctive or biologically determined behavior. The concept of culture, then, unifies all the disparate subdivisions—at least in American anthropology. It is somewhat different in British and French anthropology where archaeology and physical anthropology are usually academically separated from social anthropology—the study of social groups. (Discussions of these differences will appear in ensuing chapters.)

Academically separate or not, physical anthropology, archaeology, sociocultural anthropology, and linguistics have all contributed to the development of anthropological theory, and this book is about the development of theory as opposed to the substantive or descriptive content of anthropology.

SOURCES OF THEORY

Though many factors have contributed to the development of ethnology, it was largely the product of Western philosophy and Western historical events. Roots of current anthropological ideas about human behavior lie in questions posed long ago about the nature and origin of human beings. In early times, Europeans' ideas about man's nature were limited by partial and erroneous information and molded to suit Judeo-Christian traditional beliefs. But European perception of human diversity was broadened by descriptions of non-European cultures as a result of the explorations following Columbus' voyages. And the development of scientific ethnography at the end of the nineteenth century provided more accurate cross-cultural information for comparative purposes. This opened up a wider horizon than the narrow view from within a single society, and made possible more general testing of hypotheses about culture and human nature.

The theoretical basis of any discipline is always influenced and modified by developments in other disciplines. Thus, interaction between anthropology and other disciplines contributed information and stimulus too, and as change and advance occurred in one area, there was a kind of chain reaction into others. To give two examples, Freudian and other psychological approaches opened up new avenues of research and inquiry in anthropology, and new geological information about the age of the earth led to new hypotheses about the origins of man.

Social scientists ask questions for a purpose, usually one pertinent to the social issues of their times. Consequently, political and economic events and conditions have had an impact on theory development. And likewise, the course of Western imperialism often influenced the direction and goals of ethnology. (This is discussed at greater length in the following chapters.)

Social science, as a whole, benefited from the application of the methods of natural science. The idea of using the experimental method—hypothesis testing under controlled situations—was a bequest of the period we call the Enlightenment. Ideas and conjectures were to be verified or falsified by experience, by application of controlled experimentation to the study of man, and through the application of the scientific method. Therefore, social science gradually became less deductive and more inductive.

All these and many more influences played roles in the development of ethnology as old ideas were elaborated and reinterpreted in light of new data. Sometimes tradition restricted new developments, but often it acted as the basis for further thought. Students will see as they progress through this history that very few totally new theories occur in anthropological doctrine today, though there may be new names for them. Most are recombinations and reinterpretations of older ideas about the nature of the human animal. The result has been cumulative and expanded knowledge that has led inevitably to new questions about the ways of mankind.

Anthropological theories basically focus on questions such as, "*Why do people behave the way they do?*" and "*What causes human diversity?*" We will look at sources of theory from the past, examine historical relationships and changes in theory, and also compare continental European, British, and American views. Throughout, the aim is to see what relationships exist among past and present theories, new information, and the general political and social climate of the times. The book is arranged chronologically, showing the sequence in theory development. It starts with the Age of Exploration when European interest in non-Western peoples sharpened, and it shows the impact on anthropology of discoveries not only of new societies around the world, but also discoveries and developments in geology, biology, psychology, and economics, as well as the influence of conventional assumptions.

Students should not expect to find the one right solution to human problems or the one correct answer to social questions. *Right* and *correct* must be judged not as absolutes, but only within specific contexts which differ according to variation in their cultural settings. What seems explanatory and illuminating at one time may well be judged laughable, inadequate, or hopelessly dated at another. There are many ways of looking at facts, and none has scientific sanctity.

SOME DEFINITIONS

Before taking a look at the development of anthropological theory, it is desirable to give simple definitions for a few of the terms we will be using. First, the word *theory* itself: a *theory* is a statement of the principles presumably regulating observed processes, or one that accounts for causes or relationships between phenomena. A *hypothesis* is a provisional conjecture or contingency; a statement of plausible connections among specified elements. Generation of testable hypotheses is a primary function of theory. When confirmation is total—when the hypothesis or theory checks out 100 percent of the time—it is usually considered a *law*. (*Hypothesis* and *theory* are often used interchangeably in informal speech.)

A *generalization* is a statement that something is true or typical of a certain class of things; a statement that connects two or more things or events by their common attributes. Hypotheses and theories are both types of generalizations.

In recent years, use of the word *model* has become increasingly popular in the social sciences. A *model* is a generalized picture, analogy, or explanation of a researcher's observation. It is more of a confined statement of relationships than a theory, and an image somewhat closer to reality. Many people see no difference between the terms *model* and *theory* and consider the popularity of the former to be something of a fad.

Two other words frequently used in behavioral sciences are *approach* and *orientation*. As used in this book, they are virtually synonymous, and they mean the prominent features or criteria used by a scholar in his ideological considerations or relative emphasis in theory and method. Thus, we might refer to an historical approach or orientation. And when we speak of a *school*, we mean the disciples or followers of a particular scholar or orientation; for example, the Marxist school.

Determinism[2] and *deterministic* as used here, and in anthropology generally, refer to simplistic explanation. They imply a facile, incomplete, often bigotted and one-sided excuse, and do not offer a true explanation. "Those people are grasping; it is in their blood," is an example of biological determinism, and "People of the tropics are lazy and mentally slow," is a statement of environmental determinism.

The essence of the *scientific method* or *empirical method* is: observation, classification, experimentation, and generalization. Any trained researcher working within the same context, with the same equipment or components, should always be able to verify and duplicate the experimental results of another. Given the same data, they should draw the same conclusions. As we shall see, such ideal circumstances rarely occur in the study of human behavior.

EXPLANATION IN BEHAVIORAL SCIENCE

The ideal conditions of scientific, controlled experimentation do not exist in the science of human behavior. It is almost too obvious for comment that human beings are not molecules and cannot be subjected to conditions of laboratory testing. In ideal scientific experimentation, one component is allowed to vary; all others are held constant. Such controlled conditions are so rare in the behavioral sciences that we can say categorically that they do not exist. But even if we assumed for the moment that such controls were possible, we would still be faced with the problem of objectivity. We are literally studying ourselves, and our conclusions

[2] Be aware that the usage of *determinism* is not the same in philosophy where it refers to the theoretical stance that everything that happens is fixed by antecedent conditions. In philosophy, it is, therefore, a theory of cause at odds with a "free will" philosophy.

are always filtered through a screen of our own subjective values. All this means that we may never arrive at a point of absolute proof. Perhaps the best theoretical position we may reasonably expect is one that allows us to ask the most pertinent questions of our data.

We often speak of "explanation" in terms of *dependent* and *independent variables*. Elements that precede and produce change in other elements are called independent variables. Dependent variables are those factors which are changed or controlled by the independent variables. The greatest challenge in the science of man is to demonstrate causal relationships. Cause implies time relationships: something comes first and something else follows. Somewhat easier to show is correlation: occurrence of one component commonly associated with the appearance of another. In the long run, social correlations often must be stated in vague terms: usually, often, frequently, and so on. If data are quantified, correlations may be expressed as percentages: when X is present, Y is also present 80 percent of the time. Explanation in terms of multicausation and concomitant variation may be the most exact we can make: clusters of variables or factors may lead to a certain result. For instance, archaeologists tell us that the combination of agricultural production, population density, and occupational specialization often resulted in urban society. In anthropology, it is rare to the point of being unknown that we can say that factor A causes effect B.

In addition to causal explanations, social scientists use *functional analysis* in the interpretation of data. Instead of indicating that one element leads to or causes another, functional analysis illustrates how components work together to support the structural whole and maintain systemic relationships and continuity. Functional explanation, unlike causal explanation, requires no time sequence; it is synchronic explanation. (More will be said about functional explanation later.)

2

Prologue to Anthropology

Sociocultural anthropology, as a formal subject, is a young discipline. The first academic position was University Reader, held by Sir Edward Burnett Tylor at Oxford in 1884. However, interest in and speculation about the diversified ways of human beings have a long history, doubtless going back before writing. Although some people of antiquity (for example, Herodotus and Strabo) showed great curiosity about the customs of others—and perhaps Caesar was the first person to use the culture area concept when he divided all Gaul into three parts—the Age of Exploration is a more reasonable beginning for our short history.

THE AGE OF EXPLORATION

In the fifteenth century, Prince Henry of Portugal prepared the way for later European exploration of the continent of Africa by voyaging to Tangier and encouraging the development of navigation. In his wake in the following centuries, explorers investigated other areas: the Orient, North and South America, and the Pacific Islands. Even earlier, the Venetian merchant, Marco Polo, had written what would qualify as a pretty good ethnography of the court of Kublai Khan in Peking as it was around 1275. By 1800, Europeans had enough information to speculate about human society on a global scale.

There is little doubt that ethnography and indeed anthropology in general were affected by imperialism. European fleets not only staked out claims to raw materials, spices, and gold, but with their cannon power extended authority over the peoples of the newly discovered lands. In succession, Portugal, Spain, England, the Netherlands, and France became masters of the sea lands and built colonial empires. By the nineteenth century, practical responses by European governments and commercial interests, faced with problems of control and trade with newly conquered native populations, encouraged ethnographic data collection. Manipulation by the conquerors was easier as a result of their greater knowledge of native political and economic systems. However, imperialist preferences did not always lead to ethnographic research, and not all of the great colonial powers developed a discipline of anthropology; Portugal and Spain, for example, did not. Perhaps imperialism was necessary, but it apparently was not a sufficient condition for the creation of socio-cultural anthropology.

Church interests also played a part in accumulating information about peoples of non-Christian lands. Missionaries voyaging afar to convert the natives soon learned the necessity of speaking the language of those they wished to proselytize. Nowhere else were problems of communication so obvious and keenly felt as in religious translation. Development of the linguistics of unwritten languages received a considerable boost from the missionaries of many faiths, and a number of languages that since have ceased to be spoken were preserved in written form. In addition, missionaries, who normally spent long periods becoming well acquainted with their particular objects of conversion, recorded the lifeways, philosophies, and values they sought to change. They sometimes did this in order to better understand, and sometimes to present the horrors of heathenism to stimulate donations from the folks back home. Very slowly, as knowledge of non-Western philosophies and ideals spread, a few Europeans became conscious of the relativism of values and beliefs.

Popular Responses to Exploration

During the three centuries that Europeans explored, conquered, and colonized the rest of the world, they held the advantage in technology. European ships were constructed of timbers and beams massive enough to withstand the recoil of a heavy cannon. Consequently, Europeans were unbeatable at sea. On land too, European firearms were superior, giving them the power to inflict more damage than could be directed against them. Even where Europeans did not impose political rule, they often held economic dominance and trading advantages. This technological superiority colored Europeans' views of themselves and others and *has continued to this day to be a measurement of value in the minds of many*. Because European weaponry was superior, Europeans began to think of themselves as superior. That superiority had not only a geopolitical slant, but eventually held racial implications as well. In the nineteenth century, slogans like "whiteman's burden" expressed racist opinions, and Europeans deluded themselves into thinking that they brought advantages to the "inferiors" they conquered by presenting them with a better way of life materially, and—to European thinking—also morally. European goals came to include conquest and control of land, conversion to Christianity, and education of the natives to European standards.

The consequences of exploration on contemporary, nonscholarly European ideas were vast. Unknown up to that time, animals, plants, and peoples of exotic demeanor and custom excited European imaginations. Travel books and guides became enormously popular, and Europeans read avidly about Africans, Orientals, and American Indians, though most of the literature was inaccurate and concentrated on the quaint and curious, and not on other lifeways as legitimate expressions of human diversity. Ethnographic details were reported out of context, and few attempts at data collection were systematic or complete. Sometimes European response to accounts of foreign ways was, "That's human nature." Other times, readers perceived nothing in common with the foreigners. Without realizing it, those people were thinking essentially what anthropology taught in later times: *all humans are alike in some ways; all humans differ in some ways, and the differences are largely cultural.*

Scholarly Reactions to Exploration

Exploration and conquest also had broad intellectual and philosophical impacts. Explanations of the newly discovered diversity in human ways took several forms. Degeneration views, compatible with traditional Christian orthodoxy of monogenesis, or single origin, held that all humans were descended from one original couple, and that they all had fallen from an original state of grace. Monogenists accounted for the obvious variety among contemporary peoples by attributing differences to environmental responses and transmission of acquired traits. Though Europeans who believed in monogenesis usually saw their relationship to non-Europeans in terms of superior to inferior, nevertheless, they interpreted their common origin to mean the same potential for all people, and none was so savage or lowly as to preclude the possibility of improvement. This was not a racist view: all humans were created equal; differences were due not to inherited inequalities but to conditions after creation. But, it was an ethnocentric view: all people were judged on the basis of European values and standards.

Polygenist theories, however, contributed to racial interpretations. Such beliefs predicated several separate creations and suggested that there were a number of human species that differed in ability from the beginning. The strain that eventually produced Europeans was superior.

New interest in the nature of man inspired some intellectuals to question traditional wisdom and the worldview handed down in Judeo-Christian philosophy; no longer did they consider the church fathers and Greek philosophers infallible. In fact, some intellectuals concluded that the world of the ancients had been rather restricted, and their comparisons of Europeans with contemporary non-Western peoples as well as with Europeans of antiquity gave rise to theories of overall progress through time; theories of social or cultural evolution. It seemed quite apparent to some that progress—not degeneration—had occurred in human history and that living peoples might be used to illustrate the various sequences of development, Europeans, again, being at the acme. (No matter what the theory, Europeans came out on top.) This emphasis on progress, not of primary importance in the sixteenth century and seventeenth century, became a hallmark of social philosophy in the eighteenth. Scientific and technological progress made Europeans think that virtually nothing was beyond them, and they began to interpret the development of human history as leading to and culminating in the Europeans of their time. That is, the upper-class Europeans saw themselves that way, for they considered European peasantry little more than on a par with native peoples.

At first, interest in the nature of man and curiosity about human differences around the world produced what can only be called conjecture and speculation. Reasoning was deductive and few if any attempted to put their deductions to the test. But in the period we call the Enlightenment, theories of earlier thinkers came under scrutiny; the time had arrived for a critique of knowledge. Scholars began to see a need to test and demonstrate the adequacy of their ideas, and some proposed applying the inductive methods of natural science to the study of man. Intellectual ferment during the Enlightenment was confined to a small group, but composing that group were the intellectuals who had immense impact on the thinking of succeeding generations.

THE ENLIGHTENMENT

The period from the last half of the seventeenth century through the eighteenth was a time of widespread enthusiasm for intellectual pursuits to which the title "The Enlightenment" is often given. The thinkers of this period include men who worked in mathematics and physics, like Isaac Newton and Gottfried Leibnitz; in biology, like George de Buffon and Carl von Linné; in chemistry, like Joseph Priestly and Antoine Lavoisier; and social philosophers, like Voltaire, John Locke, and Jean Jacques Rousseau. Newton's *Principia Mathematica* and Locke's *Essay Concerning Human Understanding* expressed Enlightenment attitudes in natural and social philosophy respectively: *the universe was rationally ordered, and laws could be discovered that explained the motions of the planets and the behavior of people.*

Enlightenment thinkers were people of great mental breadth and depth, interested in many subjects, and they found each other's work and ideas richly stimulating. They also exerted vast influence on educated Europeans, popularizing new social, economic, and scientific ideas, some of which became the theoretical bases of the American and French Revolutions. Even autocrats like Catherine of Russia and Frederick the Great of Prussia carried on correspondence with philosophers and prided themselves on being "enlightened."

Though the philosophers ranged far and wide in intellectual pursuits, it is their interest in certain social questions that most concerns us. The social philosophers (we cannot yet call them social scientists) argued about the nature of man and society, ideal human behavior, causes of human behavior, and the course of human nature, among other things. They wondered and debated about the separation of nature and nurture, which of man's aptitudes and attitudes were innate, which learned, and which could be changed. Though many of their conclusions seem naive today, they laid the basis for what was to come, and in many ways the social philosophers were precursors of anthropology, or even proto-anthropologists themselves.

Eighteenth century ideas about the nature of man ran the gamut from romantic primitivism to the belief that strong monarchy was necessary to restrain people, who were inherently self-seeking. This range of ideas can be illustrated by the thinking of three men: Jean Jacques Rousseau (1712–1778), Thomas Hobbes (1588–1679), and John Locke (1632–1704). Hobbes believed that human beings were by nature brutish and selfish and that strong and repressive government was necessary to control them. Rousseau represented the other extreme. He thought that humans in a state of nature were essentially good and free but were ruined by civilization and society, and he urged a return to the "natural state." Locke concluded that humans were neither good nor bad at birth, but were "blanks," and became what experience made them. He stressed the educability of people, for good or ill, as their social environment and circumstances dictated.

Many aspects of Enlightenment social thinking have remained in contemporary anthropological theory. One lasting contribution was *humanism*, the concept of the worth and dignity of all humans. Another was the importance of education and the social environment, especially the socialization of the young. A third idea that has remained an integral part of behavioral theory was that human beings were a part of the natural universe, not special, separate beings; therefore, they were subject to the operation of natural laws that could be identified and studied. Enlightenment social philosophy thus took man out of the realm of divine creation and made him eligible as a subject for empirical inquiry. It would be difficult to overemphasize the importance of this latter point for the development of the science of man.

Although they stressed the educability of man, most social philosophers used European standards as a measure of perfectability. They interpreted historical change as progress toward European ideals, and thus bound their scientific objectivity with the chains of ethnocentrism. As they perceived human history, people had become more knowledgeable, scientific, rational, moral, and competent as they progressed toward European attainments.

This notion of progress was recent. In Greek and Roman times, as well as in the Middle Ages, the fall of man from some golden age or state of grace was taken as a matter of course. Even Renaissance people conceived of a past more glorious than their present. Well into the eighteenth century, belief in the "decay of the world" was common. In figurative terms, human society was pictured as having gone from an ancient golden age through silver and bronze ages to the final (contemporary) iron age. But developments in natural science changed all that. Suddenly it seemed that there were no limits to human capability. It was a firm tenet of the eighteenth century that progress was self-evident. Humans had improved, and improvement—progress—was infinitely possible in the future. Though some philosophers revived Platonic attempts to represent ideal behavior, most were quite sure that there was no debate. They thought their own society and way were best because they were based upon rationality and because their thought processes most closely responded to the principles of natural law. By this view, Europeans had thought themselves into a more advanced society.

All the social philosophers were greatly influenced by the spurt in natural science and the development of the "scientific method." Like mathematicians and physicists, the social thinkers sought regularities and universal laws of human behavior, for they were convinced that such existed. Just as the natural scientists perceived a world governed by mechanical laws on the model of Newton's celestial mechanics and law of universal gravitation, so those pursuing inquiry into human behavior sought behavioral laws and looked for natural causes. By applying the experimental method, they hoped to discover such laws. As in the natural sciences, they would observe phenomena, develop hypotheses, and then test those hypotheses through more observation and experimentation.

The philosophers were skeptics. Though most believed that a deity had set in motion a perfect universe, a harmonious and orderly machine, they also thought that man, once in that world, was on his own and would flourish as he observed natural law and suffer if it was broken.[1] Those thinkers were antimiracle and anti-mystic and looked for causes in antecedent behavior and not in divine interference or retribution. They blamed human problems on human beings, not on the super-natural. It was an age of inconoclasm and skepticism, and a belief in natural order governed by natural law.

Two points of Enlightenment intellectual activity were Scotland and France, where scholars, today better known for work in other theoretical areas, advanced some ideas that later became incorporated into the body of sociocultural anthro-pology.

The French Group—Three Examples

Charles Louis de Secondat, Baron de la Brede and de Montesquieu (1689–1755), known to us simply as Montesquieu, took an early cross-cultural approach to social research and included considerable human diversity in his studies. Recognizing that society was an extremely complex phenomenon, he amassed a large body of infor-mation both from his reading and from his travels through most of Europe. He observed and recorded human social behavior, collecting data for some 20 years, before he wrote *Spirit of the Laws* (1748) which was primarily a work on political and legal theory, but in addition, an inductive analysis of interacting institutions and social processes through time. In effect, it was a modern descriptive work on the origin and nature of law which he meant in the broad sense of social con-trol as a means of social integration. He decided that differences among societies arose from their various past histories, from their sociocultural frameworks, and importantly, from diversity in their environments. He emphasized environmental factors to a degree that some have interpreted as environmental determinism.

Montesquieu abandoned the ethnocentric view so commonly held among many of his contemporaries, and concluded that one society should not be judged by another's standards, but only on its own terms. He thus stated a position that, in the twentieth century, became known as *cultural relativism*. In his writing, Montesquieu suggested a classification of three developmental stages of human

---

[1] The concept of natural law played a prominent part in Enlightenment philosophy. It referred to an ideal pattern according to nature, discernible by reason, and separate from law established by church or state. Natural law was believed to provide universal rules for con-duct, for distinction between right and wrong according to nature's (or in some usages, God's) morality. It was independent of all human authority. Some philosophers maintained that no human law was valid if it was contrary to natural law. John Locke appealed to natural law to support his claim to the natural rights of life, liberty, and the pursuit of happiness.

history that was to achieve great popularity in the nineteenth century: *hunting or savagery, herding or barbarism, and civilization.*

Anne Robert Jacques Turgot (1727–1781), best known today as the French comptroller-general who tried to put national finances in order for Louis XVI, outlined a projected book on "The Historical Progress of the Human Mind" (1750) in which he suggested that mankind had gone through three stages of increasing complexity and food-getting competence. His scheme, somewhat similar to that of Montesquieu, based the stages on hunting, pastoralism, and farming. He described the lifeways he thought must have been typical under the conditions of hunting and pastoralism, and pointed out the advantages that animal domestication and agriculture offered in terms of leisure time, sedentary life, occupational specialization, and population increase.

He attributed human diversity on a global scale, not to biological differences, but to variety in education, environment, and degrees of isolation from other people, in other words, to cultural differences. He perceived the cyclical nature of development in the rise and fall of nations, and implied that though the stages of growth might vary from place to place, no one region or group of people held a monopoly on civilization.

The work of Marie Jean Antoine, Marquis de Condorcet (1743–1794) best exemplifies the Enlightenment emphasis on progress that dominated European thought. He put his faith in the limitless perfectability of human beings, and believed that the scientific study of man would clearly demonstrate advance and achievement through history to a climax in the French Revolution. He hoped some day to write a definitive intellectual history which he sketched in *The Outline of the Progress of the Human Mind* (1795). He divided history into ten stages, the last an optimistic projection of the future. It was specific rather than general, a history of European rather than human thought, and he did not live to complete the larger work.

While many writers, like Condorcet, largely ignored the geographic discoveries and ethnographic materials collected in the two previous centuries, preferring instead to use biblical and classical mythological characters for their depiction of natural man, others began to incorporate some of the newer information. Rousseau drew upon accounts of the Carib Indians of South and Central America to create his image of the "noble savage," though he greatly romanticized his descriptions. Montesquieu drew upon ethnographic data from non-Western societies and used them thoughtfully for his work on comparative political and legal systems.

The Scottish Group—Three Examples

David Hume (1711–1776), Scottish philosopher, historian, and economist, hoped to transform the moral sciences (by which he meant social sciences) as Newton had transformed physics. He argued persuasively against acceptance of miracles and maintained that knowledge could come only from observation, not speculation, and he explained many cultural similarities as the result of diffusion or cultural borrowing. He laid the basis for a psychological probe of society which he believed formed as the result of man's sexual nature, and he pondered about the mechanisms of the human mind and the impact of culture on personality.

William Robertson (1721–1793) was an historian and professor of history at the University of Edinburgh. Like Montesquieu, he pictured human society through three stages of development: savagery, barbarism, and civilization, and recognized that before metals had ever been smelted, people had used stone tools. He ascribed differences among humans to characteristics acquired through enculturation and to the effects of geography. Though he was not the first to suggest the Asiatic origin of American Indians, he used faunal and ethnographic evidence as proof of their origin and entry into North America over the Bering Strait. He considered the New World natives examples of humans in the "infancy of social life."

The work of another Scot, Adam Ferguson (1723–1816), embodied much Enlightenment thinking about the nature of man and portrayed social progress in a sequential stage development that forespoke the full-blown social evolutionary theories of the nineteenth century. In his book, *An Essay on the History of Civil Society* (1767), he emphasized the continuity and dynamics of society and tried to determine the reasons for the rise and decline of nations.

Though he did not use the word, Ferguson clearly gave expression to the concept of *culture* and recognized its many varieties which, like Montesquieu, he saw as partly due to environmental differences. He believed that man's gregarious nature arose from the long period of infant helplessness and that through socialization processes children become the kind of adults approved by their society. Ferguson explained the fervor with which each society clings to and exalts its own ways above others (ethnocentrism) as a logical consequence of long-term socialization in group values. Many of his ideas became taken for granted as social science developed in the nineteenth century.

Implications of Enlightenment Thinking for Social Science

In the eighteenth century, social philosophers began to appreciate the tremendous diversification of human society, though frequently they used non-Western groups only to illustrate people living in a state of nature that preceded civilization. Nevertheless, they created a foundation for genuine cross-cultural analysis that became feasible with the accumulation of comprehensive and accurate ethnographic data at the end of the following century.

The philosophers were interested in human origins and stressed continuity in social evolution (they called it progress). They created schemes of historical development, most of which started with Greek and Roman beginnings, both immediately ancestral to European society, and not the origins and prehistory of mankind as a whole. But the interest was there awaiting only the advances in geology and archaeology that forced revision in the estimates of man's antiquity.

Though the philosophers tried to separate biologically determined behavior from learned behavior, they never were able to explain why such variety in learned ways should exist. The result was the beginning of many simplistic and inadequate explanations, like racial and environmental determinism, that have continued to plague us to this day. Nor were the thinkers successful in their attempts to separate nature from nurture. Better understanding of biological functioning and mechanisms of adaptation was some generations in the future.

The Enlightenment thinkers began to study social institutions like government and religion; a focus still maintained in anthropology and sociology. They also viewed societies as natural systems of integrated, interacting parts foreshadowing later functional approaches to social studies. But perhaps the most important legacy from the Enlightenment to the science of man was its heritage of inquiry and stress on the application of natural science methodology to human behavior. The philosophers believed in natural order governed by discoverable laws. They discredited presumptive reasoning and examined data and conclusions in a critical spirit. The concept of a rational approach to the study of society as well as much of our contemporary social and political thought, are derived from the eighteenth century, and many democratic concepts embodied in the American Constitution, Declaration of Independence, and the French Declaration of the Rights of Man can be traced to the social philosophy of the Enlightenment.

NINETEENTH CENTURY BACKGROUNDS

The early nineteenth century was characterized by reaction to the French Revolution: *nationalism, political conservatism, a return to revealed religion*, and *literal interpretation of the Bible*. In England, evangelical religious faiths blossomed. Popular culture and thinking largely abandoned the rationalist and empirical approaches of the eighteenth century when philosophers had attacked tradition. The new spiritual attitude in the world of arts, and indeed on the part of the general public, was characterized by nostalgia for the past, especially for the Middle Ages as opposed to the Classical Age. In fact, degeneration theory experienced a kind of resurgence as many people compared their present lives unfavorably with earlier times, and emotional rather than rational interests were emphasized. In literature, music, and art, this sentiment has been labeled the *Romantic Movement*.

In the economic arena, the Industrial Revolution was in full swing. Industry expanded with almost explosive force, new technology developed apace, and the middle class, the bourgeoisie, grew along with it. So did the proletariat, but in those early industrial days, the latter was a largely powerless group. The bourgeoisie, newly rich, controlled production and finance. This class was politically and socially conservative, desirous of government protection but not government regulation, and the economic policy called laissez-faire (governmental noninterference) developed under entrepreneurial guidance. Still fearful of the radicalism that the revolutionary era had spawned, the capitalists wanted no state interference with their control over the laboring class.

The growing proletariat had few spokesmen in the early nineteenth century. Labor unions were weak, and industrialists and politicians were not concerned with the workers' welfare. Some people of the world of literature, like Charles

Dickens, some social workers, and non-professional humanitarians were almost alone in their attempts to improve the horrendous conditions of factory work. While most human beings toiled 16 hours a day for very low wages with no unemployment or sickness benefits, a few others grew vastly rich.

The general economic and political inequality caused social unrest and eventually provoked humanitarian movements seeking social reform.[2] Many troubled people called upon social scientists to study problems of economic disturbances and social disorganization in order to arrive at solutions to the generally unsettled conditions. These early attempts at social planning took many forms. Some social thinkers were sincerely convinced that the scene mirrored conditions in the animal world— a fight for existence—in which the most worthy would endure while others would perish. This can be summed up in the phrase: *the survival of the fittest*. Those who took such a position favored government nonintervention, a hands-off policy. Herbert Spencer stands as representative.

Others advocated active application of social science research and knowledge to the goal of alleviating social ills. One active participant in social planning was Claude Henri, Comte de Saint-Simon (1760–1825), who is considered by some to be the founder of the science of sociology. He viewed the industrial system and technology as needing regulation, but basically as beneficial to mankind. Saint-Simon proposed what many have classified as a Utopian scheme for ministering to the needs of the poor through distribution of salaries and inheritances and regulation of employment.

Another reformer was Karl Marx (1818–1883), who responded intellectually to the social problems of the day with an economic view of history and the nature of man. He saw the entrepreneurial class as basically self-aggrandizing, and perceived no good in the industrial system, which exploited the workers. He urged not merely the study of industrial society, but active intervention to control the activities of the capitalists.

Two other phenomena were hallmarks of the nineteenth century social scene: *racism* and *nationalism*. Some historians have called this century the "Great Age of Nationalism"; a movement highly tinged with romanticism and the intensification of in-group unity wherever it occurred. In many cases, racism and nationalism were two facets of the same state of mind: loyalty to, and exaltation of, one's own group.

Racial explanations had occurred but were not common in the eighteenth century. (By racial explanation we mean the attribution of *group* mental traits and behavioral characteristics to biologically inherited properties.) In the nineteenth century, however, there was a great increase in racist interpretation by both scholarly and popular writers for purposes like, for example, the justification of slavery. Both the monogenist and polygenist positions could be used to support racially discriminatory practices. The polygenists stated that races differed in ability because they differed in origin, while the monogenists said they differed in ability,

---

[2] Robert Owen, who agitated in the cause of factory legislation, was responsible for one of these movements: the Utopian community at New Harmony, Indiana.

though of common origin, because they had developed differently and in response to different needs. Supporters of each position failed to distinguish between learned and inherited characteristics. Nor did the publication of Darwin's theory clarify issues; increasing numbers of people, among whom we must include many who considered themselves anthropologists, accepted the idea of white supremacy as not only logical but as demonstrable. The colonial conquests of three centuries, among other things, were deemed evidence for the superiority of European civilization, an ethnocentric judgment on the basis of European standards.

Scientific Advances in the Early Nineteenth Century

During this era a number of scientists paved the way for the development of physical anthropology and archaeology. Alexander von Humboldt, a German geographer and naturalist, explored parts of South America and central Asia and studied geologic forms, plant life, and archaeological remains. He was convinced of the Asiatic origin of American Indians. Georges Cuvier, a comparative anatomist, classified all animals into four great branches, and extended his studies to paleontology and fossil remains. He believed in the immutability of species and attributed differences that occurred through the passage of time to destruction of earlier forms by a series of catastrophes and the successive creations of new species. This is a theory of development called *catastrophism*. Though he recognized and attempted to account for extinct animal remains, he denied the existence of human fossils. He belived that man had been recently created and that the "biblical flood" was the most recent of the catastrophes. He considered all evidence that disputed his thesis to be fake.

In 1797, in Suffolk, England, below approximately 12 feet of soil, John Frere, a member of The Society of Antiquaries, uncovered the bones of extinct animals in association with flints which he suggested had been worked by man at a time before he had known the use of metal. Some years later, Jacques Boucher de Perthes, an amateur archaeologist, found implements of early man in a 40-foot-deep stratum near Abbeville, France, and published his opinion that the flints had been manufactured by humans living in a very remote period called *antediluvian*, or *before the flood*. Ridicule was the first response to the report, but it was not long until scientists began to accept his conclusions.

More information leading to reconsideration of the length of human existence and the age of the earth came from advances in geology. In 1830, in *Principles of Geology*, Charles Lyell expressed the doctrine of *uniformitarianism*: action of climate, water, chemical decomposition, and internal disruptions had acted to change the crust of the earth for all time in a uniform manner. Changes, therefore, were not due to a series of castastrophies, but were due to the same causes throughout time. Just as erosion and uplift were slow processes in the nineteenth century, so they had required aeons of time to shape the earth, and, consequently, that planet must have had a longer life than anyone had realized. The past could be read in the present, and geologists had to take into consideration vast periods of time.

Those incalculable spans of time had implications not only for geology but also for archaeology. Man-made items found in deep strata of the earth and in association with fossil animal forms had to be far older than the traditional date of 4004 B. C., assigned by Bishop Ussher to the creation of man. The bishop's calculation of the date of creation had been accepted since 1650 with few questioning it; suddenly it became untenable. Europeans had traced their ancestral antiquity to include ancient Greece, but the new discoveries implied that their forefathers had lived in a far more primitive state than anything recorded in Homeric poetry. One reason public interest in ethnographic literature developed was that Europeans sought to reconstruct their own remote past by using contemporary native peoples as representatives of early stages of human existence.

Social Philosophy in the Nineteenth Century

No clear break with Enlightenment social philosophy can be discerned in the opening decades of the nineteenth century. Efforts of the eighteenth century social philosophers to apply the scientific method to the study of human society culminated in the nineteenth century in the development of sociology; a term coined by Auguste Comte (1798–1857) to replace his earlier label, social physics. He hoped to create a science of society as precise as the science of physics. Comte is best known for his philosophical orientation called *positivism*, a term derived from the title of his principal work, *Cours de philosophie positive*; the English version was published as the *Positive Thinking of Auguste Comte* in 1853.

Saint-Simon and Comte had been associates, and Comte was greatly influenced by the older man. He was also intellectually indebted to Turgot, Hume, Montesquieu, and Condorcet, among others. Perhaps Comte's greatest contribution to social science lay not in original thinking so much as in his efforts as synthesizer and systematizer of the intellectual innovations of his times and the period just preceding. He also gave to succeeding generations of social scientists an integrated body of data and theory on which to build further.

Comte believed that earlier modes of thought, which he called theological and metaphysical, were imperfect, and that positive knowledge had to be based on natural phenomena whose properties and relations were verified empirically. Comte envisioned a developmental sequence of human history; a sequence of increasing intellectual complexity that was essentially an evolutionary scheme. He saw social change primarily as mental change, spread by education, eventually resulting in human perfection in all societies as the result of increased human rationality. The Enlightenment doctrine of the *infinite perfectability of mankind* is obvious in Comte's work.

The English philosopher, Herbert Spencer (1820–1903), pictured change in human society, and also in the inorganic and biological world, in terms of universal evolution several years before Charles Darwin published his theories of biological evolution. Spencer belonged to the tradition established by Comte and attempted to apply positive science to the study of man. His central concept was evolution, or progress, for he really equated the two ideas. Throughout his life he tried to apply an evolutionary approach to every science. His universal evolutionary scheme envisioned inorganic, organic, and superorganic (or social) evolution. Nebulae evolved into planets; geological evolution produced oceans and landforms; plantlife evolved through metabolism of the elements, and society evolved from family forms into states and federations. Homogeneity evolved into heterogeneity; simplicity into complexity in all phenomena of the cosmos. Spencer considered evolution a basic unifying process and principle, and he has been called the philosopher of *universal evolution*. It seemed to him that evolution was the grand theory that could explain everything.

Herbert Spencer wrote voluminously of evolution in all fields, publishing among other things a three volume work, *Principles of Sociology* (1876–1896) in which he compared society to an organism with processes of integration, growth, differentiation, decline, and with functional interrelationships of parts in change and transformation. Spencer is well known for this organic analogy which was taken up and elaborated on by many other social scientists. His organic analogy and the application of evolution to society represent a major contribution to sociological theory.

In contrast to the antagonism that met Darwin's biological evolution theory a few years later, Spencer's evolutionary scheme was well received. The European public had no objection to the idea of social evolution, for it was obvious that society had improved (that is, progressed). Even the devoutly religious felt that after the biblical fall from grace, religion had evolved into superior forms, and no one argued that technology had not evolved. The advances of the Industrial Revolution were proof of that. History demonstrated that mankind had gone through stages of development—call it what you will, evolution or progress. C. J. Thomsen, a Danish museologist, analyzed archaeological collections according to the period of manufacture, and he established the sequence of stone, bronze, and iron ages. You will recall that in the previous century some Enlightenment phi-

Herbert Spencer, 1820–1903
(From Haviland 1975; courtesy of Holt, Rinehart and Winston)

losophers had used another classification of human development: savagery, bar-barism, and civilization. The historian Condorcet had outlined European history as a series of stages based on inventions like the alphabet and printing. Though the word used before Spencer was *progress*, the notion of cultural evolution had been present and quite acceptable for some time.

Biological Evolution

In 1858, before a learned audience, Charles Darwin (1809–1882) read a scholarly paper which outlined his theory of biological evolution, and in 1859 published his book, *Origin of Species*. The general public was opposed to the ideas he presented—in fact, it was violent opposition. Acceptance of cultural evolution did not carry over into the realm of biology. In light of the nineteenth century religious revival, the reaction was not surprising. To many, Darwin was challenging the Bible and proposing a theory quite offensive to the "faithful"; few members of the general public took time to read what he actually said. In the Judeo–Christian tradition, change of customs and institutions into more complex and advanced forms was not shocking, but such change applied to bioforms was unacceptable to those who believed in fixed, immutable, divinely created species. Cuvier's ex-planation of fossil forms, as the result of multiple creations and catastrophes, was far preferable to Darwin's explanation, which was popularly distorted to mean that humans were descended from apes.

Though evolution is prominently associated in the public mind with Charles Darwin, another man, Alfred Wallace (1823–1913), independently and virtually simultaneously developed a theory of evolution. It was Wallace's work that finally forced Darwin into publication, for, though Darwin had formulated his theory by

Charles Darwin, 1809–1882
(From Haviland 1975; courtesy of Holt, Rinehart and Winston)

1838, he had not put it into print. In 1855, Wallace published a paper in which he stated a theory of evolutionary change, and in 1858, in a letter to Darwin, expressed ideas on the mechanism of natural selection, which he believed was the basic means of evolution. Darwin read Wallace's essay, together with his own paper written in 1844, before the meeting of the Linnean Society in 1858. The two papers were published by the Society the following year.

There really was no significant difference between the theories of the two men. Thomas Malthus' work *An Essay on the Principle of Population* was instrumental in the formulation of the theories of both Wallace and Darwin. Briefly, they both drew the same conclusions from the data they had observed. Everywhere more organisms were born than lived to adulthood. Within the group, there were always small individual differences. Those individual variations supplied the reason some lived while others did not: *some were better equipped to meet the demands of their total environments.* Those better equipped lived to reproduce and pass their qualities to the next generation where the process began anew. This process became known as *natural selection.* Neither Darwin nor Wallace knew of genetic transmission; it was left to Gregor Mendel 50 years later to supply that information. But essentially Darwin and Wallace described the same idea of organic evolution by means of variation and natural selection.[3]

Social Darwinism

While much of the general public—especially the churchmen—rejected the theory of bioevolution, the scholarly community not only accepted it, but began to apply it to explain many conditions of the times. Evolutionary sentiment following Darwin in biology and others in sociology became the dominant theoretical stance. Spencer, thinking in terms of universal evolution even before Darwin published, seized upon Darwin's theory as further substantiation of what he had been saying and applied Darwin's mechanics of biochange to society. Spencer—not Darwin— coined the phrase "survival of the fittest" and claimed that in conflicts between societies, the superior replaced the inferior and in so doing demonstrated that the winners—the survivors—were the fittest. This application of the struggle for survival applied to social conditions is called *social Darwinism.*

Social Darwinism greatly overemphasized heredity and ignored learning in behavior. In the nineteeth century, social Darwinism was used to justify social status quo, imperialism, laissez-faire economics, and racism. Spencer concluded that state welfare and social planning would upset the laws of nature by which human suffering would gradually disappear as the weaker and less fit were eliminated in the struggle for survival. Social Darwinism (also called Spencerism) became a major theoretical support for free enterprise and private property because those

[3] Darwin became known as the discoverer of evolution primarily because he discovered the principle first and spent far more of his life studying and writing about it. After his initial work, Wallace became interested in other things and also antagonized the scientific world of his time by opposing vaccination. In addition, he himself gave credit to Darwin for propounding the theory which he referred to as "Darwinism," thereby acknowledging Darwin's primacy.

aware of the mechanisms of natural selection believed that government interference would upset the balance of nature. Natural selection applied to human behavior was interpreted to mean that aggression was both innate and proper. Mankind was involved in a conflict to determine the stronger and fitter race or society; the one to survive. Thus would civilization progress.

3

The Beginnings of
Sociocultural Anthropology

By the last half of the nineteenth century, agrarian, feudal Europe was dying and industrialization, urbanization, and vicious class antagonisms created social tensions of frightening intensity. A few people were beginning to question the established order and the social inequity that had seemed like part of the divine scheme of things. Various socialist movements sought to bring about change on an international scale that would eliminate social privilege and economic inequality. Anarchism, a mutant of the individualism that had marked the early century, gained popularity in many European countries and, to some extent, in America. Unlike the socialists, anarchists denied the usefulness of any sort of organization or political party in achieving their ends of freedom for the workers and the elimination of private property. They thought voluntary cooperation would replace the role of government once the existing system was overthrown.

Most social scientists remained aloof from practical applications of their disciplines, neither agitating for reforms nor engaging in social welfare activities. Accepting the basic tenets of social Darwinism, they too believed their social positions and knowledge implied and confirmed their superior fitness. English imperialism continued on an enormous scale under Queen Victoria, and France colonized almost to the same extent. In the middle of the nineteenth century, this was the background for the development of sociocultural anthropology as a systematic study of primitive cultures and societies.

THE EARLY PERIOD OF ETHNOLOGY

Anthropology, as the word was used in the early nineteenth century, was usually applied to what is called physical anthropology today. It was the study of man the animal, and in those early years, it centered on cranial comparison and measurement, and involved a great deal of speculation about superior and inferior human groups. In preDarwinian days, the study of (physical) anthropology included very little fossil interpretation, for few remains of early man were available.

Like sociology which had already become an independent discipline, cultural or social anthropology was intended to be a true science that applied natural science methodology to the study of human society. As it developed, it differed from sociology in that the latter was almost completely confined to the study of Western, industrialized man, while sociocultural anthropology, on the other hand, became largely the study of technologically primitive people living in noncomplex societies without written languages. Indeed, to many of the general public, *anthropology still means the study of primitives.*

Though first used to illustrate life in earlier times, primitive people soon became the object of inquiries on the nature and interrelatedness of human institutions. In the last part of the nineteenth century, anthropologists began to reason that to understand social complexity one should start with fundamentals that are far more easily studied in homogeneous groups of limited population than in industrial society. Noncomplex, primitive societies offered integrated social systems that were "storehouses" to be tapped in studies of cultural processes.

The goal of applying the scientific method to the study of primitive society was rarely achieved in the nineteenth century. It was not until the twentieth century that rigorous fieldwork and extended ethnographic research became standard. Those we think of as the cultural or social anthropologists of the nineteenth century seldom did any real fieldwork. They depended on the same kinds of inadequate and nonobjective sources for their information that had marked speculation of earlier times: explorers, trades, missionaries, various government personnel, and travelers. In this sense, their theorizing about human society was hardly on firmer grounds than the theorizing of the Enlightenment philosophers. Most data were ripped from meaningful context with the consequence that ethnography remained, to an unfortunate degree, the study of the quaint and curious, rarely a complete picture of a society.

However, it would be unfair to imply that all early ethnography and reports on tribal peoples were piecemeal and secondhand affairs (though most were). Fray Bernadino de Sahagun lived with the Aztec from 1529 to 1590 and recorded their language and customs. Some priceless information about Iroquois Indians of the American northeast was collected by a French Jesuit missionary, Joseph François Lafitau (1681–1746), and in the following century, a few people did extensive, firsthand investigations of non-Western societies (we have already mentioned Alexander von Humboldt). Another to record American Indian cultures was Henry Schoolcraft, a government agent for the northwestern frontier and husband of a Chippewa Indian. His major work was a six volume classic, *Historical and Statistical Information Respecting the History, Condition, and Prospects of the Indian Tribes of the United States* (1851–1857). It was a work of real scholarship, and he was among the first to introduce Indian legends and traditions to the public. Though these and a few other names (above all, Lewis Henry Morgan) stand out in nineteenth century ethnography, for the most part, contacts between Europeans and tribal peoples were of such short duration that the records are of minimal value. Nevertheless, though accurate, plentiful data and systematic ethnographic research were largely lacking in the later 1800s, enough information was available to allow some serious study of non-Western peoples and to stimulate the accumulation of more.

In the second half of the nineteenth century, many contributions to anthropological theory were made by men who cannot properly be called professional anthropologists. In fact, most were lawyers with entensive education in classical Greek and Roman languages and literature; we might call them anthropological dilettantes. They were interested in the customs of other peoples and read widely about tribal peoples of the world.

Two men of the late nineteenth century stand out above the others; one American and one Englishman. They may be considered true professionals, and each has been called at one time or another the father of anthropology. Lewis Henry Morgan, the American, and Edward Burnett Tylor, the Englishman, unlike almost all others did have some firsthand ethnographic experience. Each took an evolutionary theoretical approach in keeping with the general emphasis on evolution, and developed a scheme of cultural evolution that described states of human history from distant beginnings to the achievements of the Victorian age. Though the two were acquainted with Darwin's work, each drew far more heavily upon the ideas of human progress and perfectability of the Enlightenment philosophers and upon social evolutionary schemes of earlier thinkers, like Comte and Spencer. Using their own data collected in their travels, as well as information from many other sources, Morgan and Tylor fleshed out their schemes of human development employing living tribal peoples as examples of prehistoric societies; a practice that came to be called the *comparative method*. As mentioned in the last chapter, the comparative method had been used in the eighteenth century; in fact Lafitau, the missionary, wrote a book of comparative ethnology, *Customs of the American Savages Compared with the Customs of Early Times*. But it was Morgan and Tylor who systematized comparison for the discipline of anthropology.

Lewis Henry Morgan (1818–1881)

Ethnographic research in the United States was shaped by the existence of non-Western societies readily available for study (the North American Indians). Morgan was a lawyer who settled in Rochester, N.Y., close to communities of Iroquois Indians. He became fascinated with their customs, and later was engaged to act on their behalf in a land-grant case. The Tonawanda Reservation group adopted Morgan after the resolution of the lawsuit, and he was particularly fortunate in making friends with a young Seneca Indian law student, Ely Parker, who later became Commissioner of Indian Affairs. Parker helped Morgan make a serious study of the Iroquois, particularly the Seneca, the results of which were published as *The League of Ho-De-No-Sau-Nee or Iroquois* in 1851.

Morgan traveled widely, and he never passed up an opportunity to visit local Indian groups like the Great Lakes Chippewa. Later, he also spent time among tribes of the plains and prairies. Interested not only in ceremonies, religion, government, and material culture, but also in differing types of kin systems, Morgan began an intensive study of marriage, family, and descent patterns—kinship generally. To round out his own findings, he enlisted the help of Indian Agents throughout the United States, and later, missionaries and government personnel around the world, to record terminologies and classifications of kin. He tabulated and analyzed the information gained, and published it in *Systems of Consanguinity and Affinity* in

Lewis Henry Morgan, 1818–1881
(*Courtesy of New York Public Library*)

1871, the first comparative study of kinship systems. Though Morgan is better known for other works, many anthropologists believe that the kinship research is his greatest and most enduring contribution to the discipline.

Morgan's work with Indian cultures led to an interest in their origin and history. On the basis of common kinship patterns found in widely separated areas, Morgan believed he could demonstrate a common Indian origin, especially when answers to his kinship questionnaires confirmed the existence of similar kinship types in Asia. However, as time passed, he found the same types of kinship terminology—which he called *classificatory*, meaning that some lineal kinfolk were terminologically classified with some collaterals—in other areas, and he realized that similarity in terminology was not connected with Indian origins, but was rather, as he saw it, common to many primitive groups.

In keeping with the general evolutionary temper of his time, Morgan then suggested that classificatory systems represented an ancient form, and he attempted a reconstruction of human history using kinship information gathered, turning from a specific interest in American Indians to the general sequences of human history. The result of his labors was *Ancient Society* (1877), his most famous work and the most detailed exposition of the cultural evolutionist position in the nineteenth century. It was *Ancient Society* that codified the evolutionist position in anthropology and passed it on to later British and American evolutionary theorists and through Friedrich Engels to Marxian ethnologists.

In writing *Ancient Society*, Morgan accepted from eighteenth century social philosophy the idea that human society had progressed, become better and better, finally producing the civilization of his time. The task he set for himself was to describe the climb from primeval times to the Victorian period and to indicate the agents of change. He endeavored to correlate his stages of evolution with

development in technology, political organization, and kinship systems and terminologies. Employing the same categories earlier used by the French philosopher
Montesquieu (*savagery, barbarism,* and *civilization*), Morgan further divided the
first two into three statuses: *lower, middle,* and *upper.* He also supplied examples
of ongoing societies for each status, except the lower status of savagery, for which
he said no living equivalents could be found. By Morgan's scheme, the lower status
of savagery included the time from the beginning of human society to man's control of fire, and since he knew of no people who could not make fire at will, he
gave no examples of a typical group. He did indicate that people in the lower
status of savagery had invented language, held property in common, ate uncooked
foods, and lived in promiscuity with no real family structure. Civilization, by contrast, was characterized by the phonetic alphabet, intensive agricultural production,
and monogamy. Morgan classified as civilization not only modern European society,
but also ancient civilizations like Egypt, Greece, and Rome.

For each of the periods, Morgan charted development in technology and subsistence, family and marriage forms, and political organization, and he indicated
the invention that had marked the beginning of each new status. In the *period of
savagery,* the middle status was ushered in with the discovery of fire, and was
represented among living peoples by the Australian Aborigines; the upper status,
with the invention of the bow and arrow, and represented by the Athabaskan
Indians of western Canada; lower barbarism, with the invention of pottery and
represented by the Iroquois Indians; and so on. Morgan was not always clear in his
own mind about the cause of progress. Usually he used a technological invention to
indicate change of stages, thereby implying a materialist strategy, but in several
places in *Ancient Society,* he continued the Enlightenment theory of change through
increased rationality and referred to ideas as instrumental, ascribing, for example,
the evolution of political institutions to a few germs of thought. However, he was
clear in his opposition to degeneration and catastrophism theories. From his firsthand
knowledge, he rejected the theological explanation that primitive people of his
day had degenerated from an original state of grace, and believed instead that
civilization had evolved from earlier primitive forms similar to some contemporary
tribal societies.

He was trying to show cause and effect and to apply scientific method and
inductive reasoning to the study and interpretation of human change and development. His proofs are not acceptable today. Sometimes he forced data to fit
his theory, assuming, for example, that certain forms must have existed because
his theory required them. He appeared to ignore information he should have
used—the Polynesian accounts by Captain Cook, for instance. But more than anyone
before him, he built theory on facts, either from his own data or those from people
he trusted.

Edward Burnett Tylor (1832–1917)

While Tylor did no ethnographical fieldwork in the formal sense, he had a
questioning mind and refused to accept many of the data collected by missionaries

and travelers. He had been sickly as a young man, but since his family was wealthy, he had been able to travel in warm climates to regain his health. His experiences during a six-month stay in Mexico and other tropical regions of the New World resulted in a life-long interest in other societies, and he recognized the importance of staying long enough in one place to appreciate it from the point of view of the people themselves.

At home, health restored, he read widely of primitive and ancient societies, and in 1865 wrote *Researches into the Early History of Mankind* in which he detailed his version of human cultural development. In detail and coverage, it was no rival to *Ancient Society*. He published a far more significant work, *Primitive Culture*, in 1871. Contemporary in thought, his theoretical orientation like Morgan's was evolutionary, and he also used the categories *savagery, barbarism,* and *civilization*, though he left us no such detailed analysis of those stages. He described savagery as a time when technology consisted of stone tools and wild foods; barbarism as the beginning of agriculture and metallurgy; and civilization was ushered in with the invention of writing. In Tylor's scheme, civilization also indicated advance in happiness and certain moral qualities, attributes that Morgan did not include.

Tylor's special interest was the evolution of religion; the entire second volume of the two volume *Primitive Culture* concerns itself with it. The origin of religion, as he saw it, was the belief in spirit beings which he thought must have been a universal response to certain universal experiences: death, dreams, and reflected images. Those common occurrences would inevitably produce a concept of duality: spirit and flesh; image and reality. Tylor coined the term *animism* to mean belief in spirit beings, and in typical evolutionary form, he depicted a sequence from animism to polytheism to monotheism.

Edward Burnett Tylor, 1832–1917
(From Haviland 1975; courtesy of Holt, Rinehart and Winston)

Primitive Culture discussed not only animism and the origins of religion, but also defined *culture* in a way not incompatible with its current use as "that complex whole which includes knowledge, belief, art, morals, custom, and any other capabilities and habits acquired by man as a member of society." In brief, Tylor, the Englishman, gave American anthropology *culture*, its basic unifying concept, and one which British anthropologists have for the most part not found very useful; while Morgan, an American, was the founder of detailed kinship study, the British forte.

Tylor also developed the concept of *survivals* which became important in the evolutionary reconstruction of past societies. By survivals, Tylor meant customs or institutions that had lost their function but had been carried on into a later stage of society by force of habit. They continued in forms like children's games, riddles, and various superstitions. Tylor pointed out survivals even in the most advanced societies; in England they appeared in good luck pieces, for one instance. He took such survivals to indicate remnants from a past stage and proof that English society had passed through earlier, primitive stages.

Morgan found Tylor's concept of survivals useful in his evolutionary scheme. He believed that the kinship terminology by which ego calls father and father's brother by the same term was a survival from some remote age when there was no regularized marriage; that is, from the early statuses of savagery. Morgan believed that such terminology proved that at one time children knew the identities only of their mothers and called all men who might possibly have been their mothers' mate by the same term. Thus the terminology as a survival lent weight to Morgan's contention that matrilineality was a logical early descent pattern.

Though emphasizing parallel and independent evolutionary sequences, Tylor (and Morgan too, for that matter) never ignored diffusion. He was especially interested in the great resemblance between games played in Mexico and South Asia (variants of one we know as Parchesi), and questioned whether anything that complex could be invented twice, suggesting rather the possibility of diffusion. "Civilization," he wrote, "is a plant much more often propagated than developed."

Tylor is responsible for yet another creative idea in anthropology. Although the concept was not seized upon until many decades later, Tylor advanced comparative studies with his investigation of associated traits, or as he called them, *adhesions*. Tylor used a sample of several hundred societies and tried to calculate the relationships between such elements as descent rules and residence patterns. In this computation, he was ahead of his time; not until the mid-twentieth century were such adhesions (correlations) again attempted.

Both Tylor and Morgan used living tribal peoples as examples of prehistoric societies—the comparative method. It should not be confused with cross-cultural comparisons. The label "comparative method" is used to designate the nineteenth century practice of equating living noncomplex societies with extinct groups. In the twentieth century, anthropologists reacting against the practice called it the "example of the contemporary ancestor or living fossils." However, the nineteenth century theorists found no fault with the idea and used it freely. Morgan and

Tylor tended to use the comparative method more carefully than others of their time, much as anthropologists today employ ethnographic analogy (a useful method of archaeological interpretation), and they attempted to compare groups at the same level of sociocultural complexity.

Other Nineteenth Century Ethnologists

Morgan and Tylor were supported in their historical reconstructions by other contributors to ethnological thought. Though only one could be considered a professional anthropologist and none did systematic field research, all were well versed in classical studies and the ethnography of their time. These men retained and expanded the eighteenth century interest in institutions, especially the family, religion, and law, and in general explained them in terms of their origins and development. In many instances they saw anthropology as a kind of history, and the word *history* often appeared in titles of their books. Their primary focus was on human similarities or universals, and they sought social regularities with respect to broad trends, not specific events or personalities.

Adolf Bastian (1826–1905)   Bastian, a German trained in law, science, and medicine, became curator of ethnology in a Berlin museum in 1868. He had spent many years in travel as a ship's doctor, a position that enabled him to visit many lands and people virtually unknown to Europeans of his time. He was impressed by similar customs he found in widely separated places and attempted to account for them by what has been translated into English as the *psychic unity of mankind*, *Elementargedanken*, or universally similar elementary ideas. By psychic unity he implied that all humans had the same psychic or mental processes that produced similar responses to similar stimuli, but which appeared as local variants in response to differing local conditions. Bastian thought that psychic unity caused the kind of independent but similar manifestations that others might account for by the process of diffusion. He believed that diffusion operated only in the more advanced societies, not among primitive peoples, and should always be proven and never assumed. He also believed that any group had the innate capacity of independent, parallel invention and might achieve civilization given the proper stimuli or conditions.

Bastian himself was not properly speaking a cultural evolutionist, but his concept of psychic unity was adopted and applied by most evolutionists. The reason we say he was not truly an evolutionist is that he saw growth in terms of psychological givens, the development of innate forms; not organic transformation. In fact, he rejected Darwin's work in biology. Some anthropologists have considered Bastian's position to be a kind of psychological determinism. But psychic unity was used by the evolutionists to explain why some societies were hung up in the past while others forged ahead to civilization. The former merely awaited the necessary stimulus.

Johann Jacob Bachofen (1815–1887)   Bachofen, a Swiss lawyer and classical scholar, discovered references in classical mythology to early matrilineal societies preceding Greece and Rome. When he found data about other matrilineal·societies in ethnographic literature, he developed the theory that matrilineal societies must have existed universally during a primeval period of sexual promiscuity; while no one could be certain of his father's identity under free sexual activity, the nature of mammalian reproduction always identified the mother. Consequently, he reasoned there must have been an early period of mother-right or matriarchy which was replaced in a later period when men became desirous of passing property on to their own children. That desire prompted men to overthrow mother-right and institute instead patriarchy with strict monogamous marriage so they could be certain of the identity of their heirs. Matriliny remained among some primitives as a survival from earlier times. Bachofen published these conclusions in *Das Mutterrecht* (Mother-right) in 1861. His reasoning was widely accepted, and Morgan's interpretation that matrilineality preceded patrilineality, made on the basis of kin terminology, supported Bastian's position.

John F. McLennan (1827–1881) McLennan, a Scottish attorney, was fascinated by evolutionary ideas about the institution of marriage. Though his starting point was somewhat different—his interest had originally been aroused by ethnographic reports of bride capture, a practice he was familiar with from his classical studies— he too added to the development of social organization theory. Like Bachofen, he reasoned that an early stage of group promiscuity resulted in matrilineal descent. During the early stages of mankind, female infanticide must have been a common practice because, as it appeared to him, females were useless in military and hunting pursuits and a drain on the food supply. The scarcity of women resulting from female infanticide was resolved by bride capture and polyandry—multiple husbands. The practice of a woman living with a group of brothers (fraternal polyandry) then resulted in patrilineal descent reckoning. In civilization, bride capture remained as a *survival* in the practice of carrying the bride across the threshold.

McLennan's hypothetical reconstruction of the evolution of social organization had less impact on anthropology than theories of the others mentioned, but in his discussion of marriage patterns in his book *Primitive Marriage* (1865), he coined the terms *endogamy* and *exogamy*, still used to indicate the rules of marriage within the group and outside the group, respectively.

Henry James Sumner Maine (1822–1888) Maine, an English jurist, took quite a different view of social evolution. His major anthropological work was *Ancient Law* (1861), in which he described sequences in the evolution of law. On the basis of his extensive knowledge of antiquity, and (east) Indian society, he concluded that descent patterns had not evolved from matrilineal to patrilineal. His research indicated that in the most ancient times, Greek, Roman and (east) Indian societies had been patriarchial and no evidence of any prior matrilineal stages existed. Maine's primary interest was in the evolution of law, and the sequence he suggested was a continuum rather than a series of stages: organization on the basis of kinship evolved into organization on the basis of territoriality; status into contract; inalienable land to salable land; and civil law to criminal law. He suggested that changes differed from society to society, and there was no single sequence through which all had gone or must go.

General Evolutionist Position

The general nineteenth century evolutionist position (often called *classical evolutionism* or *unilineal evolutionism*) may be summed up as follows: The evolution of culture or society proceeded through a single line of development, with set stages of similar content for all people, though the pace of development varied from society to society. This unilineal sequence reflected the psychic unity of mankind. Everyone responded in a similar manner whenever they encountered the same stimulus. Though some evolutionists, Morgan and Tylor, for example, recognized the action of diffusion and believed it possible for some societies to leap whole stages, the unilineal aspect was very prominent in classical evolutionist theory.

The presence of survivals (vestigial patterns from the past which had lost their functions) was taken as proof that societies had gone through earlier stages. Morgan applied the concept of survivals to kinship terminology to support the contention that matrilineality had preceded patrilineality. The methodology of the nineteenth century evolutionists was the comparative method—reconstruction of past behavior through the use of living tribal people as examples of earlier stages.

By and large, the classical evolutionists believed in the doctrines of social Darwinism, which was the application of biomechanisms of natural selection to society. Social Darwinism indicated that some societies and individuals were better equipped than others to rule or dominate, and it also justified imperialism. In extending authority over other cultures, European nations merely demonstrated their fitness, and their right to command and control. Those who did not survive perished because they were culturally inferior, and because they could not compete, in Spencer's terms, in the *survival of the fittest*.

Later Extensions of Classical Evolutionism

Though classical evolutionism reached its high point in the nineteenth century, no sharp break with its doctrines occurred at the turn of the century. Some important people in early twentieth century anthropology were associated with evolutionism. One of them, Sir James Frazer (1854–1941), was in his day the anthropologist best known to the general public, and his reputation was enormous.

Frazer never did any fieldwork and is often exemplified as the typical "armchair anthropologist"; a person who developed his theories solely on others' ethnographic research. He was, nevertheless, an extraordinary scholar. Best known today for his work on mythology, *The Golden Bough*, published in 12 volumes by 1915, he ranged from comparative religion and magic to marriage, kinship, exogamy, and totemism.

Frazer was convinced that mentally all primitive peoples were irrational, and that superstition rather than empirical knowledge guided primitive thinking. He proposed a three stage evolutionary sequence from magic to religion to science. He also pointed out that the average "civilized" person accepted science with as

Sir James Frazer, 1854–1941
(*Courtesy of Pitt Rivers Museum,
University of Oxford*)

little basic understanding as the primitive person accepted magic. That is, they both took the beliefs on faith rather than on the basis of scientific testing and knowledge.

His distinction between magic and religion was that magic is manipulative while religion is supplicative. This is still quoted, as indeed are his definitions of two laws of *sympathetic magic*. The law of similarity states that like things influence each other, and the law of contagion states that things once in association will continue to influence each other even when apart. Both these principles are demonstrated in manipulations with a voodoo doll.

Popular though Frazer was, new approaches to ethnology were clearly in the air by the last decade of the 1800s in both England and America. The new approaches were largely a reaction to the abuses of classical evolutionism, though in attempting to remedy faults of the nineteenth century theorists, many anthropologists overreacted and as will be discussed later, created a new dogmatism in turn. However, before considering the twentieth century, two other important nineteenth century developments must be considered; developments that influenced the thinking of succeeding generations of anthropologists.

KARL MARX (1818–1883) AND FRIEDRICH ENGELS (1820–1895)

Marx had intended becoming a teacher after his education at the University of Berlin, but he could not find a position because of his unorthodox political views. He worked as a writer and editor of a newspaper for a while, then went to Paris, the center for socialists and others interested in working-class movements. With Engels, the son of a wealthy cloth manufacturer, he participated in the founding of the Communist League in 1847, and in 1848, the two men coauthored the *Communist Manifesto*, which presents the Marxist view of social evolution.

Engels not only wrote with Marx, but also authored many Marxist works alone. His clear literary style, far easier to read than Marx's own pedantic prose, popularized Marxian concepts. In addition, Engels provided financial support for Marx who devoted his later years entirely to research and writing.

Marx differed from other social philosophers of his time in that he encouraged action programs as means to the goal of eventual ownership by the state. State control could occur only after the abolition of private property, which he saw as inevitable and which he believed would come as the result of revolution in a highly industrialized state. He condemned social scientists for remaining aloof from social problems and not engaging in active social reform.

Marx's theory of class struggle reflected both the dialectic idealism of the philosopher Hegel and the process of natural selection which Marx learned from Darwin's work. While Hegel viewed development arising from a conflict of ideas (thesis, antithesis, synthesis), Marx based his evolutionary scheme on materialist conflict between social classes, focusing on the means and modes of production peculiar to each period. He believed that every society evolved into a new system as the result of internal struggle between interacting, competing forces, and he further argued that material causes and economic conditions were the determining factors, or the independent variables.

The theme of Marx's critique of capitalism was that the inherent contradiction between increasing material wealth and the deepening poverty of the workers would cause the breakdown of the system. His historical analysis showed that since the Industrial Revolution, workers had changed from independent producers to hired and propertyless factory hands dependent upon the entrepreneurs who owned the means of production and became rich on the profits derived from the workers' products.

The Communist Manifesto was published nearly 30 years before Ancient Society (1877), but when Marx and Engels read Morgan's book, they found independent validation of their theories. It seemed to them that examples given by Morgan substantiated both the dialectic approach and the historical materialism of Marxian philosophy. Until they became aware of Morgan, Marx and Engels had confined their work to a study of class society, overlooking nonliterate peoples and, therefore, not including the full range of human societies in their research. Morgan gave new depth to Marxian theory. Marxian explanation was materialistic, and one reason Marx and Engels found Morgan to be so significant was because Morgan's was a materialistic strategy quite consonant with theirs.

When Ancient Society appeared, Engels especially found it so provocative and conclusive that he wrote a book titled Origin of the Family, Private Property, and the State that was almost a summary of Morgan's work. Engels wrote it, of course, not as anthropology, but in order to point out how Morgan supported Marxian tenets. Through Engels, Morgan became an honored theoretician in Soviet ethnology. Even when evolutionism fell from favor in Britain and America, it remained an accepted theoretical approach in Russia because of the impact of Morgan and Engels.

Engels adopted Morgan's position on the origin of the family. He accepted as fact that from an original promiscuous horde, matriliny developed only to give way eventually to patriliny. Monogamy was the marital form of civilization. But unlike Morgan, he said that monogamy as it developed was only for women and represented oppression of the female sex by the male through practice of the double standard. Monogamy, he further stated, was based not on natural but on economic conditions, and he proposed that social organization was determined by both the stage of development of labor and the stage of development of the family. In early stages when kin groups dominated, labor was less specialized and social wealth was limited, but as productivity increased, differences in wealth and private property arose with accompanying class antagonisms. Social control at that point could not be effectively carried out by kin groups. Consequently, a new form of social grouping based on territory developed: the State, which implied a police force maintained by taxation. Civilization represented the *State stage of development*. One must read *Ancient Society* along with Engels' book to appreciate the degree to which Engels' evolution is derived from Morgan.

However, Marxian evolutionary theory was not competent anthropology; it was too speculative and concerned itself with wishful thinking. Its faults were those of the classical evolutionists: it was too deductive and prone to the errors of the comparative method and the concept of fixed stages. In the twentieth century, anthropology took a twist in another direction toward data-gathering and inductive analysis. This was definitely a healthy change, and Marxian philosophy had little impact on anthropology in western Europe or America until mid-twentieth century.

EMILE DURKHEIM AND FRENCH SOCIOLOGY

French monarchy twice replaced democratic government in the nineteenth century, and the Third Republic, emerging after the insurrection and Paris Commune of 1871, was an unstable, fragile thing. Class antagonisms were rampant, and flagitious anti-Semitism boiling over during the Dreyfus Affair[1] became increasingly violent not only in France but throughout Europe in the late nineteenth century. It seemed as though France was being torn assunder.

Considering the general social scene, it is understandable that Emile Durkheim's (1858–1917) primary concern was with the beliefs and symbols shared by members of a society. He wanted to understand and explain the nature of *social cohesion* (or *solidarity*, as he called it) and what bound people together. Developed under Comte's impetus in the early part of the century, sociology in France took a new, vital turn when Durkheim sought cross-cultural data on which to base his studies of social development, suicide, religion, and above all, social cohesion. Though sociologists claim Durkheim as their own, his cross-cultural approach has led many

[1] Alfred Dreyfus, an officer in the French Army, was court-martialed for treason in October, 1894, on the basis of evidence later demonstrated to be false. The case became a famous cause involving anti-Semitism and other issues which were made public by Emile Zola, Georges Clemenceau, and Anatole France, among others. Eventually Dreyfus was completely exonerated.

to consider him as much anthropologist as sociologist. He denied the utilitarian explanations popular in economic theory of his time: that self-interest in pursuit of wealth or happiness bound individuals together into a functioning society. He questioned whether industrialization brought greater happiness, even though over-all wealth increased. According to Durkheim, it was impossible to measure anything like happiness, and he pointed out that no society composed of totally self-seeking individuals could exist. He concluded instead that social cohesion was the result of the binding moral force arising from participation in a common system of belief and values; a system which molded and regulated individual behavior.

Durkheim called the shared ways, beliefs, and sentiments rising from common experiences and interactions among members of a society the *collective conscience*, a translation from the French which does not carry the French meaning quite accurately. The French word *conscience* has connotations of both conscience and consciousness in English, and collective conscience means common awareness and understandings. Durkheim never hit upon the concept of culture, and he used the clumsier term, collective conscience, to mean much of what we imply by culture. In distinct contrast to the Enlightenment philosophers, who saw man as a thinking animal and rational master of his fate, Durkheim perceived the collective conscience as controlling each member of society from birth. According to Durkheim, rather than people making society, it was society that made people social.

Unlike Marx, who emphasized struggle and opposition, Durkheim focused on normality, stability, and solidarity within society. Though his main interest lay in understanding contemporary society and its problems, Durkheim turned to a study of traditional society for comparison and tried to understand the difference between collectivity in primitive society and in industrial society. He concluded that in primitive society, the bonds were based on kinship and common socialization patterns, a type of cohesiveness he called *mechanical solidarity*. Mechanical

Emile Durkheim, 1858–1917
(Courtesy of The Bettmann Archive)

solidarity is typical of societies where parts are essentially the same and inter-changeable. Individuals replicate each other, and segments of such societies can break away, but still the society can function. In industrial society, individualism has developed but people still need each other because they have become occupa-tionally specialized. Consequently, social ties have changed from kin-based to economic complementarity and interdependence, or what Durkheim called *organic solidarity*. Again we see a contrast with Marx who believed that increased differ-entiation resulted not in functional interdependence and cooperation, but in com-petition and strife.

In the shared ways and beliefs of a society, Durkheim saw a separate, distinct level of reality: the level of social behavior, a category to which Spencer's term, *superorganic*, is often given. Durkheim thought that though the shared patterns have no existence apart from the individuals who compose society, they could not be explained in terms of individual behavior. To explain them by psychology, biology, or environment would be the equivalent of explaining the organic phenomenon of an animal in terms of its chemical components. Social behavior to Durkheim was more than the sum of all individuals participating in society and could not be reduced to the desires and drives of those individuals; the whole could not be understood by reducing it to its parts. To do so would be reductionistic.

How then does one study behavior of people in society? Durkheim condemned earlier social theory as proceeding from ideas to things, and he wanted to produce a truly scientific methodology for the study of social phenomena. He proposed the *social fact* as the unit of analysis. A social fact may be treated scientifically like something concrete. It is recognized by its pervasiveness in society—that is, it is common and widespread, not individualistic—and by its obligatory nature—it is coercive; people feel obliged to observe its constraints.

Social facts are the norms, common expectations and understandings, and be-havioral rules that exist prior to the individual's emergence into society, and that the individual observes as a member of society. Social facts may be ignored by people at times (at their peril), but nevertheless, they are recognized by those composing the society as proper or right. Neglect of, or indifference to, norms threatens the solidarity of society and produces a state of normlessness or *anomie*, when old standards and rules have lost their meaning, and nothing else has taken their place.

Explanation of social facts themselves must be sought in other social facts. They too are part of the level of social phenomena, not individual psychology, and they are caused by other social facts. Durkheim denied that either race or environment was causal. Causation, as he saw it, came from internal, not external factors.

Durkheim took a functionalist approach. He analyzed institutions, organizations, and beliefs to see their interrelations and how they worked together to maintain social solidarity or cohesiveness. To explain a social phenomenon (or social fact), he said, it is not enough to know its cause; we must find the function it fulfills, and both cause and function must be sought within the social milieu. His work, *Suicide* (1897), clearly shows his functional approach. In it he examined the interrelationship between the incidence of suicide and other social traits like church membership and marital status. Social life, as he saw it, was the functioning of the social structure. He insisted that *function* be distinguished from *purpose*, because purpose implied individual intent, which to him was a reductionistic explanation, denying, as he did, that social facts were created consciously by individuals. Though Durkheim used functionalism to explain certain phenomena rather than as a consistent theoretical framework, he is usually credited with influencing the development of the functionalist schools in British social anthropology in the twentieth century.

In the later years of his life, Durkheim turned to a study of religion; a work that influenced many scholars. Turning to ethnographic literature of Australia and the practice of totemism which he assumed was the most basic, simple form of religion, he concluded that ritual and belief reflect society; that indeed, the object of worship is society itself. His last book, *The Elementary Forms of the Religious Life* (1912), presents his thesis. He discriminated between the sacred and the profane, the nonnatural (or supernatural) and the natural, the former being set apart from daily life by special rules and provisions. Observations of those rules and common beliefs united the devotees into a single community. In other words, religion was a major aspect of the collective conscience. Religion was a binding mechanism with profound social functions.

PROFESSIONALISM IN FIELDWORK

Around the turn of the century, anthropologists came to realize that their dependence upon ethnographic data from nonprofessional sources severely limited their research. A number of men who had been trained in the natural sciences entered the discipline of anthropology and recognized the importance of making their own systematic collection of data in the field. Some seminal work was done by teams, for example, the British Torres Strait Expedition (1898–1899) with Alfred C. Haddon, a zoologist; William H. R. Rivers, a physician and psychologist; and Charles G. Seligman, a pathologist, among others. Though none of these participants was initially trained in anthropology, they all became professionals. In this country, Franz Boas, at that time associated with the American Museum of Natural History, launched the Jesup North Pacific Expedition (1897–1902) to study the specific questions of relationships and connections between peoples in northeast Asia and those in northwest America. Boas had previously lived with the Baffin Island Eskimo, originally to do a geophysical study, and among Indians of the northwest coast.

The expense involved usually precluded mounting teams of fieldworkers, and it became more common for a single researcher or a pair to go to the field. Walter Baldwin Spencer and Frank J. Gillen (neither a trained anthropologist) did fieldwork among Australian Aborigines at various times between 1896 and 1901. Their collection of information was the basis of Durkheim's analysis of religion (*supra*) and is still recognized as the major pioneer study on the peoples of central Australia.

The various field expeditions amassed data showing clearly the value of doing one's own research from an anthropological point of view, and they also pointed out errors in many nineteenth century assumptions like the belief that primitive people had very rudimentary forms of marriage—or none at all! The early field-workers usually used interpreters and often stayed only long enough to ask questions, but as the twentieth century advanced, so too did the conviction that more extensive fieldwork was essential for professional anthropologists. Soon student anthropologists were expected to remain to learn the language and establish rapport and intimacy with the people.

The most influential theoretical advance from the early field experiences was Rivers' formulation of the *genealogical method* and his delineation of concepts like descent, which became immensely important in the analysis of kinship. The genealogical method itself was a byproduct of Rivers' research in heredity. In order to trace biological characteristics through several generations, Rivers recorded pedigrees of the natives. In time, he observed that the collection of these genealogical data gave him an unexpected amount of sociological information on kinship and general social relations. Today, the taking of genealogies is a standard fieldwork procedure even when kinship is not the focus of study.

4

The Early Twentieth Century

As the twentieth century opened, disillusion was in the air. Many thoughtful Europeans began to think that the promise of science had somehow been betrayed. Social problems had not been solved, and it seemed that greater material and industrial progress for some was concomitant with increasing poverty and deprivation for millions. It was apparent now that human resources had been wasted and natural resources inequitably distributed. While some Europeans believed they bore the burden of imperialism, in their own countries they could not shoulder the problems of underemployment and inequal access to power. Maybe social Darwinism was wrong after all—certainly the doctrine of the *survival of the fittest* began to seem restricted to material, not moral, strength. A few started to wonder what right or reason they had to assume superiority over the native or tribal peoples of the world.

By 1910, it became obvious that 40 years of European peace was approaching an end. Seemingly out of control, the European nations moved toward the most destructive conflict the world had ever known, and before it was over, the United States had been drawn in. At the end of World War I, nearly 9 million lay dead, but the British Empire was vaster than ever. The addition of former German territories in Africa, German New Guinea, about 100 Pacific Islands, and Mesopotamia and Palestine brought the Empire to 450 million souls, representing nearly every race and religion in the world. School children learned that the sun never set on the British Empire.

The exact relationship between anthropology and colonialism is warmly debated. In many ways, ethnography in the early twentieth century was shaped by general political and economic concerns and problems of the times. Money supporting research usually came from government departments or from vested economic interests. In the United States, anthropological attention focused on the American Indians, while British anthropologists turned their attention primarily toward the people of the British overseas lands. Americans, including various agencies like the Smithsonian, wanted to gather as much information about the fast changing, or even disappearing, native societies as possible. The British responsible for colonial peoples tried to accumulate information on native social and political organization that would make the task of control easier for the conquerors and less oppressive for the conquered.

The British minister in charge of running the Empire operated out of London and rarely had firsthand experience with the peoples for whom he was responsible. Direct experience was left to the bureaucracy of civil servants in the field. However, most District Officers, who spent many years with the people, were so busy with the practical matters of governance that they had no time for theoretical and comparative studies. (R. S. Rattray, an official who did outstanding research on the Ashanti, is a notable exception.) Neither had they the training, nor in most cases, the inclination for research. They were concerned with the welfare of native populations, but in general they regarded the people as children needing paternal guidance.

Consent lay at the base of British colonial rule. To hold down those millions by force would have required an impossibly large army. Wherever possible, the British built up the prestige of the local chief and used him as a government agent without trying to detribalize or Westernize the society or give the people a share in the administration or decision making.

Sometimes ethnographic data supported the British government policy by supplying information about tribal institutions, especially social and political organizations, though the anthropologists did not consider their research primarily for government use. However, in the early twentieth century, to gain recognition and support for the discipline, some anthropologists urged their usefulness as people who could help colonial officials understand the ways of the subject peoples. For example, the Royal Anthropological Institute supported the establishment of an anthropological teaching center for colonial officers and merchants on the basis that expensive misunderstandings could be avoided for a fraction of the cost of military intervention. It is probably accurate to say in both Britain and America anthropologists believed that good ethnographic information would help government personnel avoid mistakes that might be not only costly but also painful and destructive to native peoples. Whether such attitudes demonstrate that anthropology was a "child of imperialism and colonialism" contributing to a "heritage of exploitation," as is sometimes charged, depends upon one's point of view. What is unquestioned is that many members of the socalled Third World came to distrust and dislike anthropologists in an abstract sense, seeing them as self-serving researchers using data gained from fieldwork, not to help those they studied, but for their own professional advancement in the academic world. One American Indian commentator (Deloria 1969) blames anthropologists for the policies and programs that vex Indians. However, anthropologists have countered his contention by pointing out that basic policies were developed long before there were any anthropologists in the field, and many British and American anthropologists have deplored the fact that their governments have never asked their advice or have never taken it when profferred.

ANTHROPOLOGY BEGINS TO DIVERSIFY

Before the nineteenth century had run its course, some anthropologists were objecting to the unilineal evolutionist scheme. In America and Britain, small groups of professionals spoke out against the abuses and inadequacies they perceived in classical social evolution. On both sides of the Atlantic, greatest objection arose to the ethnographic data used by the evolutionists: the data were too frequently unverified and taken out of meaningful context. The nineteenth century theorists had been too deductive and had elaborated their sequences on the basis of too little substantive information. They frequently assumed what they were trying to prove and forced facts into preconceived categories. The objectors pointed out that there was no proof of evolutionary stages, no proof that the reconstructions were accurate, that the classical evolutionists generalized far too readily, and that they were ethnocentric in their judgments. The critics asserted that the psychic unity concept was obviously wrong because there was a wide range in human responses to the same situation. Finally, since it appeared that culture was in fact borrowed more frequently than it was invented, how did diffusion fit into the evolutionary stages? The evolutionists had largely ignored the processes of diffusion and migration.

In the twentieth century, while continuing support for evolutionism was represented by Frazer and a few others, one can discern four general reactions against that position: an extreme diffusionist stand that was almost entirely British; the Austro-German historical-diffusionist school; American historicism; and British structuralism and functionalism.

Extreme Diffusionism

The extreme British diffusionists were not professional anthropologists. The main figure was Grafton Elliot Smith (1871–1937), an Australian[1] anatomist and surgeon of high reputation who had gone to Egypt to pursue anatomical studies on mummies. While there, he was impressed with the ancient Egyptian culture and technology. He concluded that civilization was so special a combination of traits that it could not have been invented more than once. Unaware of the societies of the Tigris-Euphrates area that preceded Egyptian development, Smith assumed that Egypt was literally the cradle of civilization which had then spread from that country to the rest of the world, becoming diluted as it diffused.

The impulse behind civilization according to Smith was religion and he believed that the concept of afterlife and the practice of embalming were critical stimuli to man's quest for more than mere subsistence. He contended that the complex of irrigation agriculture, sun worship, pyramids, mummification—all of which could be found in New World societies in the Andes and Meso-America—was proof of the great chain of diffusion from Egypt. His emphasis on sun worship and large stone monuments gave the names *heliocentric* or *heliolithic* to his school, which included William J. Perry (1887–1949), a school headmaster and author of *Children of the Sun* (1923). Perry's work was widely read and generally believed

---

[1] *British* is not confined to *English* as many Americans mistakenly believe. It includes those from Scotland and Wales as well as New Zealanders like Raymond Firth and South Africans like Max Gluckman. However, it does not include (when applied to social anthropology) Canadians who are considered part of the American anthropological tradition.

by the public, and while professional anthropologists have always pointed out the inaccuracies and inadequacies of the extreme diffusionist thinking, the theories continue to receive public attention.

Although W. H. R. Rivers started his anthropological work in the evolutionist persuasion, in his late career he declared for a diffusionist-migrationist position. It is really unfair to classify him with the extreme British diffusionists as some have done for Rivers' theoretical stance was tempered with fieldwork, and he did not arrive at such rash conclusions as Smith and Perry. He did, however, analyze the Melanesian culture area in terms of migrations of populations and he believed, like Smith and Perry, that dilution or deterioration of traits occurred as they diffused; the Australian Aborigines being examples of immigrants who suffered technological degradation. Rivers' reputation does not rest with his migration-diffusion historical analyses but with his kinship and psychological studies.

Austro-German Diffusionism: Kulturkreislehre (Culture Circle Theory)

Far more accurate and scholarly than Smith's and Perry's work was research on the problems of diffusion and migration versus invention done by members of the Austro-German culture historical (*Kulturhistoriche*) school. Though they too thought that mankind was basically uninventive and that diffusion and migration had been too greatly ignored by the classical evolutionists, they did not fall prone to the errors and wild suppositions of Smith and Perry. The *Kulturhistorische* theorists gave anthropology a respectable body of theory even though it has had little impact in the United States and Britain. The Austro-German approach was through analysis of culture complexes identified geographically and studied as they spread and developed historically. It had, consequently, both time and space dimensions.

Friedrich Ratzel (1844–1904), founder of anthropogeography or cultural geography, while not actually a participant in the Austro-German school of anthropology, did give it impetus with his work on migration and his studies of the differing reactions of old inhabitants and new immigrants to the environment. Ratzel's student Leo Frobenius (1873–1938), Fritz Graebner (1877–1934), and Wilhelm Schmidt (1868–1954) were the important figures of the Austro-German school. Convinced of the general uninventiveness of human beings, they worried over the problem of how to demonstrate diffusion and migration. Eventually two major tests emerged, translated as the criteria of form and quantity. The criterion of form proposed that similarity of form not arising from the inherent properties of an artifact must indicate an historical connection between two items, though from widely separated geographical areas. The criterion of quantity postulated that great similarity in complexity or many parts in common might be used to validate presumed diffusion. Such criteria were far easier to apply to material culture than to traits of social organization or religion, but for Graebner, that was no drawback, for he was associated with a museum and worked primarily with material culture. The problem that these men never quite solved was the degree to which complexity must exist to indicate that it is unlikely that independent invention occurred.

Some things must be taken to indicate contact; Robert Lowie gave the example of a Gothic cathedral in the Kalahari Desert which would have to be taken as proof that Europeans had been there. But some ideas seem to be virtually ubiquitous, certain designs like scrolls and spirals, for example, and their presence in widely separated areas, proves nothing.

Schmidt was responsible for the final elaboration of the developmental scheme also employed by Graebner and Frobenius. They postulated that a few original cultures spread out from the point of origin in time and through space like ripples on water to produce *all* world culture. To the ripple effect of the culture growths they gave the name *culture circles*, which provided the title by which the Austro-Germans are best known: *Kulturkreisschule*, or culture circle school. Since this scheme of circles was one not only of diffusion and migration, but also development in time (each original culture went through developmental phases), they produced what many have perceived as an evolutionary scheme even though the men objected to classical evolutionism.

THE RISE OF CULTURAL ANTHROPOLOGY IN AMERICA

Though Lewis Henry Morgan was a seminal thinker whose prominent place in the discipline of anthropology will never be questioned, professional anthropology in America developed under the sponsorship of another man, Franz Boas, a scholar of demanding standards and great charisma—a number of his students called him "Papa Franz."

Franz Boas (1858–1942)

Boas, born and educated in Germany, wrote his dissertation on the color of sea water and received a doctorate in physical geography from the University of Kiel. While pursuing geographical studies in northern Canada, he lived among the central Eskimo, and his fascination with their ingenious adaptations to the rigors of arctic life caused him to turn from geography to the study of anthropology. He

Franz Boas, 1858–1942
(Courtesy of The Bettmann Archive)

read the nineteenth century classical evolutionists, and from his background of physical sciences, soon realized the tenuous nature of the ethnographic data on which they made such sweeping generalizations. Boas did not refuse to accept the idea of evolution—indeed, he thought biological evolution scientifically proven—but he objected to the many lapses from scientific validation to which the cultural evolutionists seemed oblivious. Evolutionism had become a stale approach and was applied too narrowly as well as too broadly; narrowly as when it was argued that art must have evolved from representational to conventionalized to abstract; too broadly in the establishment of indiscriminate generalizations about human history.

Boas saw that anthropology needed a new framework but he avoided all broad theorizing until better and more complete information was available. In his early years as a teacher, he encouraged his students to collect as many ethnographic data as possible—total recovery was his goal—and to avoid generalization and comparison until a large body of such data existed, at which time he believed theories would emerge more or less on their own. Backed by undisputed facts, he hoped eventually to be able to generalize about human behavior. However, toward the end of his life, he came to the sad conclusion that it might never be possible to generalize meaningfully. There were simply too many variables which he saw as the result of individual psychologies and unique historical events.

Instructions to his students included accumulating all data, taking the holistic approach that is one of the hallmarks of American anthropology, and emphasizing the wide variety of cultural ways, plurality, and divergence. While the evolutionists had searched for similarities, Boas looked for diversity and some of his critics have complained that his insistence on detail prevented him from seeing the total picture.

Boas did not ignore history in his attack on the evolutionists. In fact, he focused on specific histories, believing that each society could be understood only in light of its particular past. Each culture, he thought, was a unique product of discrete historical events and circumstances. His historical approach pictured cultures as historical accidents with too many combinations and permutations for generalization about causation and cultural differences. Because of this stance, the term *historical particularism* is often applied to Boas and his students. He believed that the best explanation of a cultural fact was a preceding historical event, and he used the fact of convergence—similar cultural forms arising from unlike antecedent events—as demonstration that generalized causal explanation was difficult, if not impossible. Boas wanted to confine time depth to specific societies, and he opposed the assumption that cultural evolution had followed a fixed sequence applicable to all societies. His focus was on cultures, not universal culture, and his objection to the classical evolutionists was not that they attempted historical reconstruction, but rather that they did so on too few data and put living tribal people into categories of prehistoric folk—the comparative method. Boas pointed out that the tribal peoples of the world had histories just as long as civilized peoples and that their ways of life had coherence and validity of their own.

In Boas' German intellectual background were influences from Adolf Bastian, Alexander von Humboldt, the pathologist Rudolf Virchow, and the diffusionism and impact of migration and isolation on social forms of the geographer Ratzel. In addition, Boas' attention to the inside view of culture as the native saw it and his historical particularist approach seem to owe much to Wilhelm Dilthey, a philosopher with a mentalist-historical approach to the study of social science.

American anthropology under Boas developed several characteristics in addition to the historical study of particular societies. Boas was a scholar of broad interests and he urged study in the full range of anthropology. He taught and did research in linguistics, physical anthropology, and some archaeology in addition to extensive ethnography among Northwest Coast Indians. He inculcated this breadth of interest in his students—especially his earliest.

Boas found Tylor's concept of culture a useful, unifying device and he and his students so popularized its use that American ethnology and ethnography became called *cultural anthropology.* He was adamantly opposed to any biological, racial, or environmental explanation of human behavior. Boas and his followers saw the individual shaped by cultural factors, the adult being a product of his enculturation process. Consequently, they are often considered cultural determinists.

Boasians called *culture* the major unifying concept of anthropology and compared its importance to the concept of zero in mathematics. Consequently, it is surprising to learn that there has been much professional difference of opinion over its meaning. As one anthropologist expressed it, it is as though mammologists were not agreed upon the definition of "mammal." The student interested in the range of definitions and descriptions applied to the concept should consult Kroeber and Kluckhohn (1952), but here are a few examples:

Man's extrasomatic means of adaptation.
The man-made part of the environment, including the nonmaterial aspects, laws, beliefs, and so on.
Knowledge, belief, art, morals, law, custom, and any other capabilities and habits acquired by man as a member of society.
An organization of conventional understandings.
Learned as opposed to innate behavior and products of learned behavior.
Shared ideas and socially inherited assemblage of practices and beliefs.

The definitions may be separated into two major categories: *realist* and *idealist.* The realist approach is through observed manifestations, behavior, and the products of behavior. The idealist approach is through the researcher's interpretations of the culture bearer's ideas of societal values and norms. In brief, by one definition, culture is observable, by the other, inferred.

Is culture real or merely an abstraction from reality? Does it exist or is it only in the mind? The ethnographer's definition of culture affects the way he does his fieldwork and interprets his data later. For the idealist, culture is the idea of an artifact, but not the artifact itself; it is the design or mental code for proper behavior. It has been argued that culture by the idealist definition is practically impossible to verify since it is ascertained not by observation, but only by inference. On the other hand, observed patterns are always filtered through the observer's own enculturated perceptions and thereby distorted. The problem of two views of culture was finally tackled in the 60s when an attempt was made to discriminate between the two approaches.

Under Boas, then, American anthropology became characterized by a holistic approach that included prehistory and physical anthropology and the intensive study of specific cultures with the goal of total coverage—the complete description of social organization, art, religion, folklore, and other aspects of culture, as well as what could reasonably be reconstructed of their history. He stressed long, intensive fieldwork to gather the necessary information while living and interacting with the people and urged that his students learn the language better to get the inside picture of the culture.

Cultural relativism—the position that all values are relative and there are no universal standards—was another Boasian heritage to American anthropology. Boas argued that there was no culture-free means by which societies could be compared and that consequently no one could say that one society was more or less advanced than, or superior to another. Good and bad, superior and inferior, were meaningful only within the terms of a culture and could not be used cross-culturally. Cultural relativism also stressed that people like and want to continue the way of life they grew up in regardless of what it might seem to those reared in another tradition.

Cultural relativism resulted in the mid-century in an extreme posture among some Boasians who decried the use of words like "primitive" because they saw such terms as pejorative. Instead of primitive, for example, they suggested "nonliterate," meaning people without writing. Even "preliterate" was unacceptable, implying an inferior stage from which people would pass to a higher phase, a revival of the set stages of the classical evolutionists. In some ways, Boas' later students were more rigid in their cultural relativism than he himself and in the 60s, objections to cultural relativism arose. Many saw the doctrine as an anthropological evasion of responsibility for changing the conditions in the emergent nations or the Third World. (This point will be discussed later.)

Boas was immensely influential during his lifetime and for several decades thereafter. He imparted the characteristic flavor to American anthropology and during the first half of the century virtually every major figure in American ethnology was his student or a student of one of his students. Almost without exception they held him in high esteem and defended his work against detractors. His insistence on rigorous fieldwork and accurate data was sorely needed and American anthropology would have been quite different in content and approach had Boas remained a geographer. Nevertheless, the inevitable reaction came and there were many criticisms: Boas had no analytic level, only the folk level in his work; he caused a stagnation in social science explanation; his refusal to generalize resulted in sterile "trait list" anthropology; and he constrained his greatest students through the shackles of particularism.

Clark Wissler (1870–1947)

An important construct in American anthropology has been the culture area concept. Though it had been used by Otis T. Mason and by some American historians describing regional adaptations of settlers moving across the continent, it is Boas' colleague, Wissler, with whom the concept is usually associated because he so expanded and elaborated on the basic idea. Wissler and Boas were advisers for displays of North American Indians at both The American Museum of Natural History and The Chicago Field Museum. In their opposition to the use of evolutionary stages, or the Three Age classification, they renounced the display techniques of comparative artifacts popular in European museums. Neither did they wish to group the Indian collections by language families, so they decided to arrange the artifacts by region as a means of classification.

Usually, as Wissler pointed out, neighboring cultures are alike, and he called an area of similar cultures a *culture area*. He made no attempt to explain the cause of similarity beyond the historical fact of diffusion within a limited region and the common subsistence base of an area. His first culture area scheme for North America was based on food regions: bison, maize, caribou, salmon, wild seed, and intensive agricultural areas. In addition to its application to museum exhibits, Wissler found the area concept useful in organizing his books on Indian cultures, and in time he changed from a classification by subsistence to a more general one of culture traits. Material traits were far easier to map, while religion, social organization, and the like were often found not to coincide perfectly with the material aspects. Yet, in general, there was large correspondence and anthropologists later applied the culture area concept to other continents and island regions of the world.

Wissler also plotted what he called the culture center, that area with the greatest concentration of the most typical traits of the whole region. He added time dimension with his age-area hypothesis: older elements have the wider distribution and the probable site of origin is that which shows the greatest concentration of the trait. The latter found some acceptance as a relative dating device in archaeology.

Various studies mapping the distribution of elements were done by scholars and students—one of the best known was the presence or absence of traits of the Sun Dance of the Plains Indians plotted by Leslie Spier. Detractors have charged that most studies of this sort were not very productive, leading only to trait lists and distribution charts, a sterile, nonexplanatory approach. However, the culture area is useful for limited generalizing and for indicating degrees of diffusion. As an explanatory model, though, it left much to be desired until the notion of culture as adaptation was suggested in midcentury. It was a purely descriptive device as the early Boasians used it.

Wissler also attempted to delineate "universals" of culture, which are classes of culture traits that all cultures possess. In a sense, he was merely making a more inclusive trait list; in another, he was trying to bring order and classification to the rather shapeless conglomerate that was culture. He suggested that the following categories were common to all cultures: language, material culture, art, mythology and science, religion, family and social organization, property, government, and war. These nine categories were what he called the universal culture pattern. Missing from this list is a cultural characteristic the early Boasians generally ignored: economic exchange (Wissler included production under material traits).

Alfred L. Kroeber (1876–1960)

After Boas himself, the dean of American anthropology was Alfred L. Kroeber, first student to receive a doctorate under Boas at Columbia University. Upon finishing his degree, he moved to California where he soon took a position at the University of California and built up one of the great departments of anthropology in the United States.

Kroeber was a versatile anthropologist who taught and researched in kinship theory, archaeology, linguistics, and cultural anthropology. His great ethnographic contribution was the exhaustive study of the Indians of California. Kroeber broke to some degree with the Boasian tradition by looking for cultural regularities. Observing certain widespread patterns, or cultural occurrences, especially historic cycles in the arts and philosophy as well as the rise and fall of political power, Kroeber hoped to find some causal explanations.

In 1917, he published an article, "The Superorganic," in which he professed a turn to a superorganic approach that found little favor among most other Boasians of his time. Kroeber also studied changes in women's clothing fashions, concluding that there were discernable regularities that could not be the result of individual decision. His stand was quite similar to Durkheim's position that social explanation could not be reduced to individual psychology. Kroeber said that individuals were unimportant in understanding culture change and other cultural phenomena and that cultures could be understood only in terms of interacting cultural patterns and

Alfred L. Kroeber, 1876–1960
(Courtesy of Lowie Museum of Anthropology, University of California, Berkeley)

historical events. Those patterns or configurations in effect controlled individuals. He contended that culture made the genius or great man, not the other way, and inventors could discover only those things permitted by their cultures. For example, Bach, born in tribal society, could not have written a single sonata.

Kroeber supported his position by pointing out the frequency of simultaneous, independent inventions which proved, he said, the existence of cultural forces beyond the individual. A number of Boasians accused him of reifying culture—making it a thing with a will—but Kroeber remained steadfast in his superorganic position until 1948 when he modified it somewhat, stating that he had decided that "culture was *primarily* intelligible in terms of itself, not *only* in terms of itself."

Kroeber was also a configurationist. For some purposes he found the concept of culture too unwieldy and inclusive, and he sought a means of ordering data or classifying or characterizing societies by their basic patterns. The idea behind configurationism is that each society has a cluster of characteristics that mark it as different from all others. Kroeber suggested that such configurations could be seen in terms of style or in the dominance and persistence of other cultural aspects. It was an attempt to create a typology to define or identify a culture.

Kroeber added new dimensions to the culture area concept by correlating environmental conditions with native American cultures. In a detailed study, *Cultural and Natural Areas of Native North America* (1939), he mapped vegetation, physiographic, climatological, and cultural areas and gave the impetus to cultural ecological studies that were later developed by a number of his students.

Robert H. Lowie (1883–1957)

Another student of Boas' early years, Lowie made major contributions to the ethnography of American Indians, especially Indians of the Plains. Theoretically, he took issue with evolutionism in an attack on Morgan's book, *Ancient Society*, and in rebuttal wrote *Primitive Society* (1923). Typical of the twentieth century reaction to the evolutionists, in this book Lowie denied the validity of independent parallel evolution, yet at the same time, he presented some very good arguments for the development or evolution of clans (though, of course, he did not use the word *evolution*). He pointed out that clans functioned in the transmission of property rights and cooperation in economic ventures. On the basis of the age-area hypothesis he proposed that the wide distribution of the nuclear family would indicate it to be a very old institution, not more recent than the clan as argued by Morgan. In other words, Lowie showed that there were regularities in the development of social organization, but characteristically, Lowie, like other Boasians of his time, pursued causation no further, preferring instead to write more descriptive pieces and await more ethnographic data before theorizing.

In *Primitive Society*, Lowie referred to civilization as a thing of shreds and patches, a planless hodgepodge, a description that seemed to mean that he saw no integration or consistent patterning within culture. But that is a misinterpretation of his meaning which has dogged his reputation ever since. Lowie meant that

Robert H. Lowie, 1883–1957
(*Courtesy of Lowie Museum of
Anthropology, University of
California, Berkeley*)

civilization was the end product of many elements from many diverse sources. The restrictions against generalizing under which the early Boasians labored caused him to seek explanation primarily, if not solely, in terms of history, seeking cause in prior events in that particular culture. He was imbued with the Boasian thesis that each culture was unique and the product of historical accident.

Lowie stands as a distillation of the early Boasian school. He wanted to make anthropology an objective, scientific discipline, but he felt strongly that cultural explanation came only from preceding, unique events. He thought the evolutionists had failed because they ignored rigorous data collection before theorizing and because they overlooked the significance of diffusion and convergence in creating cultural similarities. Though he perceived cultural elements as interrelated (in spite of his shreds and patches comment), he saw their relationship as the result of historical events. He carefully distinguished between describing relationships and specifying causes for them and he strongly advocated more ethnographic fieldwork, for it not only uncovered vital data, but also corrected past misconstructions and misinterpretations. It was his own fieldwork among the American Indians that showed him errors in Morgan's work.

Other Early Boasians

Space does not permit more extended discussion of Boas' students of his early years, but under strictures against premature theorizing, their contributions were almost entirely in ethnographic data collection. They number among their ranks such figures as Leslie Spier, A. A. Goldenweiser, John Swanton, Paul Radin, Elsie Clews Parsons, and Ruth Bunzel. Other Boasians who branched out theoretically like Ruth Benedict, Edward Sapir, Melville Herskovits, and Margaret Mead will be mentioned later.

THE DEVELOPMENT OF BRITISH SOCIAL ANTHROPOLOGY

American anthropology developed under the direction of one man, Franz Boas; in England, two men, Bronislaw Malinowski and A. R. Radcliffe-Brown, were instrumental in the creation of British anthropology. They were contemporaries acquainted with each other, but they were rarely in England at the same time. Consequently, there was little active face-to-face competition between them and many of the outstanding younger British anthropologists of the early century were students of both. They also both taught in the United States in the 30s—Malinowski at Yale, and Radcliffe-Brown at the University of Chicago—and exerted considerable influence on American students.

Bronislaw Malinowski (1884–1942)

Malinowski was born in Cracow, Poland, and like Boas, he came into anthropology from the physical sciences. He received his doctorate in mathematics and physics from a Polish university. About the time he completed his degree he read Frazer's *Golden Bough* and became so interested in anthropology that he abandoned natural science and went to England for postgraduate study in anthropology. He acquired another doctorate, a D.Sc., this time from the London School of Economics. He then went to the Trobriand Islands to pursue ethnographic research and spent most of the war years there.

During his stay in the Trobriands, he developed field methodology to a high degree of professionalism. While Boas recognized the importance of fieldwork and encouraged long-term ethnographic experience for his students, it was really Malinowski to whom we owe the concept of participant-observation. He believed that to understand another society one must be immersed in its lifeways, participating in whatever is suitable and possible, and carefully observing the interaction and behavior of members of the society. Use of the native language is essential and the sojourn in the field must be long enough to span seasonal variations in activity—the ideal is a minimum of one year's stay. Malinowski used his Trobriand field notes as the basis for ethnographic publications for two decades; in fact, he has been criticized for extrapolating too widely on the basis of data from that one society.

As a result of his long stay in the field, Malinowski saw the integration of Trobriand society to an extent probably not possible in a shorter time. He concluded that no matter how strange or awkward a custom, institution, or trait might appear to the outsider, it had meaning and performed some task or function within its cultural context. A corollary of this observation was that no functionless traits existed—traits could not outlive their functions.

Bronislaw Malinowski, 1884–1942
(Courtesy of Pitt Rivers Museum, University of Oxford)

Malinowski saw culture functioning to satisfy the basic drives or needs of individuals who composed society; social institutions were responses to needs. He recognized primary needs—those which arose as a consequence of survival requirements—and classified them as biological, psychological, and social. All humans must eat to maintain life and must procure necessities of existence; they must operate within social groups for purposes of reproduction and raising new members of society. From those primary needs, Malinowski showed that derived or secondary needs arose with all the force and intensity of the primary needs. Though all humans must eat, *what* they eat is culturally conditioned and people everywhere have substances that are tabooed as food, though they may be nutritious. Humans respond to the primary needs most of the time through cultural mechanisms within organized groups. Other animals, which also have survival needs, respond by instinct and unlearned, patterned behavior that is genetically transmitted and species specific. Malinowski insisted that all traits and institutions were integrated into the cultural system and he pointed out that contrary to the implication of Lowie's hodgepodge of shreds and patches, order and organization existed in cultural systems.

In his many publications, Malinowski arranged his data within this theoretical framework. Unlike Boas, he looked for regularities and sought to fit particulars into the cultural whole. His most famous work, *Argonauts of the Western Pacific* (1922), showed how a seemingly bizarre institution, the kula ring of economic exchange, fitted into the social setting and satisfied primary needs. He denied that understanding a society required any historical explanation. In opposition to the Boasians, he insisted that it did not matter how forms came into existence or developed but only how they functioned.

Malinowski defined *institution* as a group of people organized for a purpose with the means of carrying out that purpose. He believed that the family was the fundamental institution and his interest in the family and in psychology directed his attention toward Freudian oedipal theory. He came to the conclusion in *Sex and Repression in Savage Society* (1927) that the Oedipus complex in its classical form was not operative among the Trobrianders who had matrilineal descent patterns; therefore, the complex was not universal as Freud had suggested. He further analyzed religion functionally as a response to survival needs, giving sanction to cultural norms, bringing comfort under stress, and explaining events for which there was no other cultural explanation.

Malinowski's main attack on the classical evolutionists was directed against Tylor's concept of survivals—those traits that endured from earlier society but lost their functions. He insisted that there were no nonfunctioning aspects to culture. He also opposed the evolutionists' search for origins and historical reconstructions and considered such a search as being worthless in functional analysis because the crucial question was how the aspects of culture functioned, not their past forms. He strongly agreed with the Boasians that the nineteenth century schemes were too deductive and that more rigorous and extensive fieldwork was necessary.

Alfred Reginald Radcliffe-Brown (1881–1955)

Radcliffe-Brown was born and raised in England and attended Cambridge University where W. H. R. Rivers was one of his teachers. At college he was considered quite a radical. He turned to anthropology for his graduate work and was influenced to some degree by Frazer but to a much greater extent by Comte and Durkheim. He did his major fieldwork in the Andaman Islands between 1906 and 1908 and some later work in Australia between 1910 and 1912. He was seemingly not well suited temperamentally for ethnographic work and his fieldwork was more survey oriented than participant-observation: colleagues and students described him as aloof and reserved.

Alfred R. Radcliffe-Brown,
1881–1955
*(Courtesy of Pitt Rivers Museum,
University of Oxford)*

Theoretically, Radcliffe-Brown had greater and longer lasting impact on the succeeding generations of British scholars than Malinowski; however, it is to Malinowski that we give credit for the development of the basic fieldwork technique. Radcliffe-Brown urged intensive field research, though he was not a particularly successful or penetrating fieldworker himself.

The two men were similar in some respects and quite different in others. They probably saw the differences more keenly than their students or colleagues. Radcliffe-Brown's anti-evolutionist stand, like Malinowski's, involved a synchronic approach. He said that the evolutionists should have looked for social laws, not for origins, and concluded that anthropology was properly comparative sociology—that is, the study of society cross culturally. While Radcliffe-Brown was not opposed to the judicious use of properly documented history, he was quite against the reconstruction of culture history that the Americans under Boas were doing; he called it conjectural history and thought it was as valueless as the speculative reconstructions of the evolutionists.

In his major ethnographic study, *The Andaman Islanders* (1922), Radcliffe-Brown used the concept of culture but in his mature work concluded that culture was not a helpful construct. (Like the Americans, Malinowski used the concept.) To Radcliffe-Brown, culture was an abstraction—values and norms of society which could never be observed; therefore, a science of culture was impossible. He preferred to limit his universe of research to *social structures*; underlying principles of organization among persons and groups in society or the set of actual roles and relationships that could be observed. Though *social structure* is not always used precisely as he defined it, and though *social organization* is sometimes used synonymously with *social structure*, Radcliffe-Brown put the basic stamp on British anthropology with his emphasis and thinking. It is because of the force of his orientation that British anthropology is often categorized as "social" anthropology in contrast to American "cultural" anthropology.

Radcliffe-Brown's aim, then, was to study social structures and formulate laws governing social behavior cross culturally. His technique of study was to determine how the parts, institutions, roles, and so on functioned to maintain the whole. He was not concerned with how the parts and wholes had developed. His attraction to Durkheim showed up in his attempt to determine how the parts were integrated to support the whole and in his argument that social facts required explanation in terms of social laws, not in the psychology of individuals.[2] Radcliffe-Brown stated that the task of anthropology was to classify societies and compare them so that generalizations might be made. Since the important processes were maintenance operations that functioned to sustain the structural whole, Radcliffe-Brown's approach is often called *structural-functionalism*, while Malinowski, who saw cultural elements functioning to support individual needs, is usually considered simply a *functionalist*. To neither man were the processes important in evolutionary or historic terms, for developmental sequences neither enlightened nor explained. To

---

[2] Note the contrast with Malinowski who was actively seeking psychological explanations and trying to understand institutions in relation to individuals.

them real explanation was functional which, as their detractors have pointed out, is not causal explanation.

Radcliffe-Brown's attack on evolutionism took the specific form of kinship study. He questioned Morgan's interpretation of the bifurcate merging and Hawaiian terminologies (which merged father and father's brothers into a single category) as indicating an early period of matriarchy or matrilineality and he also pointed out the confusion between those two terms. He suggested that kin terms could be interpreted functionally as labels of expected behavior or traditional role behavior and presented this argument in the article, "Mother's Brother in South Africa" (reprinted in *Structure and Function in Primitive Society*, 1952).

Radcliffe-Brown, like Malinowski, agreed that institutions, roles, and relationships must be studied in context—that the whole system is articulated and integrated. Like Durkheim, he used the organic analogy to explain his *structural-functionalism*, indicating the operation of organs in the integration and maintenance of the whole organism.

FUNCTIONAL ANALYSIS

Functional analysis is not limited to anthropology. It holds a respected place in all behavioral sciences, medicine, and the physical sciences as well. In addition, functionalism is characteristic of contemporary architecture and furniture design, holding that the purpose of objects should be apparent. In anthropology the functional approach is primarily associated with Radcliffe-Brown, Malinowski, and their students.

Two implications are associated with the functionalist approach. One is the purposive or teleological aspect of functionalism: that everything has some purpose; for example, the purpose of a knife is to cut. This aspect is easy to see in material culture. In a museum, for example, one hears the questions, "What is it for?"; "What does it do?" In terms of social organization, one may argue that the purpose is the perpetuation of society.

Another implication of functionalism is integrative: that the elements are interacting within an integrated whole and that they are structured to maintain the whole. As a corollary of this point there is the additional implication that the whole is affected as parts change or disappear. There is a ripple effect or a chain reaction that is much the same as the mathematical use of the word *function*; $y = f(x)$: as x changes, so does y.

As functional analysis became widely used in anthropology, it became apparent that there were two levels of abstraction involved: the purpose or intent of members of the group and the significance or utility for the society itself as perceived through scientific observation. An example of those two levels of function will clarify this point. As far as people harassed by drought are concerned, the purpose of, or reason for, a rain dance is to bring rain. Scientific analysis of the same activity would conclude not that the dance did indeed bring rain but that it united people in the face of adversity (drought), created a feeling of union in common endeavor, and acted to relieve anxiety through group action. The sociologist, Robert Merton, called the former (the folk purpose) the manifest function, and the latter the latent function. Clyde Kluckhohn, among others, found this discrimination useful in anthropological analysis.

Critics of functional analysis are fond of pointing out that the synchronic quality of functionalism precludes explanations of causality or causation requiring time depth—the effect following the cause. However, functionalists have never claimed that they gave causal explanations. The point is that there are several theories and functional explanation may be quite as enlightening for some needs as causal explanation is for others. Nor does functionalism rule out comparison and in fact there is no logical reason to rule out the time element just because the British functional approach was synchronic. Changes in function over time may be studied.

Another point of contention in functional analysis has been the implication that in a functioning whole there are no dispensable traits; all elements support the whole. If that is true, does it mean that poverty, war, crime, and other such characteristics have a part to play? Liberals, especially Marxists, have been unhappy with this interpretation. In an attempt to clarify this point, new terms have been coined: *dysfunction* and *eufunction*. Dysfunctional (*dys*, a Greek prefix meaning bad or difficult) traits tend to cause cultural stress or imbalance. Eufunctional (*eu*, a Greek prefix meaning good or advantageous) traits are positively adaptive. But, as many have pointed out, the function of any element may be at the same time both positive and negative depending upon those involved, their social position, and the circumstances; what is a state of equilibrium in one instance may be a state of social disruption in another. The aim of functional analysis is to describe the interrelatedness of elements of a cultural system without involving a value judgment of those components. However, for reformers and those directing social change, the awareness that change in one sector may have severe repercussions in other sectors cannot be neglected; and that is the essence of functionalism.

Finally, the charge has been made that the functionalist orientation of the British anthropologists blinded them to disturbances colonization had wrought and caused them to see the conquered peoples, artificially maintained by the European power, as societies frozen in time. It had also been claimed that functionalists, under the influence of a relativist philosophy and the liberal posture that all societies were equally valid, believed it was wrong to interfere with any culture: change could only corrupt the particularly vulnerable tribal people, who should be protected as "museum pieces." However, even if the functionalists did take this position—and not many by any means did—the fact is that it was not favored by colonial administrators who definitely did not adhere to a relativist philosophy but rather had little doubt that European ways were in every way superior to non-European ways. If anything, the administrators were of an evolutionist persuasion, were little influenced by any functionalist orientation, and found little use for anthropological studies.

Nonetheless, it is true that the functionalists largely ignored the effects of imperialism on tribal peoples. It is also true that their studies were not well rounded but focused specifically on social and political organization and religion, and very few studied the implications of colonialism in terms of employment, urbanization, racial interaction, or the like. But to what degree can such oversights be attributed to the theoretical stance itself, for it did not develop as a result of the British Empire but was a heritage from Durkheim and even from some earlier theorists.

DEVELOPMENTS IN FRANCE

The First World War wrought particular havoc on Durkheim and his followers. Durkheim lost his son, a war casualty and a promising young social scientist, and he himself died in 1917. Of those left of the Durkheim school of sociology, the most important ceased following up on much of his research and turned instead to editing for publication the unfinished works of Durkheim and members of the group killed in the war. Three men made small but important contributions to ethnological theory: Marcel Mauss, Arnold van Gennep, and Lucien Levy-Bruhl, who was not so much a disciple of Durkheim as a colleague in philosophy.

Marcel Mauss (1872–1950)

Mauss was Durkheim's nephew and outstanding student. He collaborated with Durkheim in *Primitive Forms of Classification* (1903). To the neglect of his own work, Mauss edited for posthumous publication the unfinished manuscripts of Durkheim and others, but he still found time to advance cross-cultural research methodology and make a contribution to economic anthropology. In this last area he demonstrated the significance of gift exchange in creating binding relationships among people and showed that such exchange has important extensions beyond the economic system into political, religious, and social sectors of society. In *The Gift* (1954), he pointed out functional ramifications of the kula ring that had escaped even Malinowski. Mauss did this analysis making comparative studies by using ethnographic studies already available, not through his own fieldwork. *The Gift* and *Primitive Forms of Classification* influenced the thinking of Levi-Strauss in the next generation.

Arnold van Gennep (1873–1957)

Gennep, another French scholar to work from material already published, analyzed rituals accompanying changes in status during critical periods of the life cycle that he called *rites de passage*. In functional manner, van Gennep showed how such rites fit into the larger social matrix and he classified them as rituals of separation, transition, and incorporation. Separation ceremonies ritually cut a person off from one status; transition rites celebrate the change; and rites of incorporation affirm a new status. Cross-cultural study of status changes and associated ceremonials had never before been done and van Gennep's work, published in English as *The Rites of Passage* (1960), still stands today as the definitive theoretical analysis.

Lucien Levy-Bruhl (1857–1939)

Levy-Bruhl was a professor of philosophy whose major interest lay in the nature of thought. Somewhat unfairly, he is known in anthropology for conclusions that are no longer acceptable about the thinking processes of primitives. He considered that primitive mentality was qualitatively different from the mentality of western peoples. He called primitive thought "prelogical" (not illogical) and said it differed from the thought processes of his intellectual contemporaries in that it did not clearly discern between cause and effect. According to Levy-Bruhl, primitive thought was imbedded in collective representations of the native societies—societies having no concept of logic or empirical enquiry. Levy-Bruhl has often been misunderstood and his detractors have made something of an intellectual reactionary out of him. He meant nothing pejorative; just that principles characterizing Western thought did not appear to be present in native thinking which functioned on different premises consistent within themselves but not including ideas of verification and testing. As many social scientists—the Durkheim group among others—were quick to point out, scientists are also a part of their own social matrix and it is not at all difficult to demonstrate that outside their professional work, scientists often fail to think logically.

5

Anthropology at Mid-Century, 1930–1960

The Great Depression following the crash of 1929 marked the change from post-World War I to pre-World War II periods. The rise of Hitler and German authoritarianism was bolstered by the economic problems of Germany and the world. Hitler had a ready answer to the question of who caused Germany's troubles: the Jews, Slavs, and other "inferiors." He aimed to purge the German nation of these races of people and many German scientists, among them some physical anthropologists, supported his efforts with data to "prove" Aryan superiority, thus falsifying the belief that those who profess anthropology are necessarily liberal.

Though the British Empire was at its peak, the handwriting was on the wall. Many of the colonies and overseas dependencies joined in the war effort only upon assurance of independence afterwards and British anthropologists were forced to grapple with problems of change as structure-breaking crises made the synchronic approach valueless.

Like World War I, World War II broke down established social patterns and customs with the end result that many parts of the world underwent fundamental political change. Self-determination became a fact rather than just a principle. In the late 40s, independent states of the Philippines, Pakistan, India, and Israel were created and many other new nations declared their independence in the following two decades: Libya, Tunisia, Republic of the Congo (Zaire), and Nigeria, just to name a few.

European political domination was thrown off but while geographic and political imperialism waned, economic imperialism often expanded. Western businessmen moved in with western goods, in many cases displacing traditional artisans and merchants and agricultural routines were often disrupted and economies of native societies endangered. Economic imperialism often engendered as much antagonism as political imperialism.

Throughout the world urbanization and its problems increased and the agricultural sectors of society decreased. With scientific advances in agriculture, it took only a small proportion of the population to feed the urban society with the consequence that many left the land for city pavements. Traditional relationships between city and country, urbanite and peasant, producer and consumer began to break down.

American anthropological research expanded into new regions geographically, into Oceania and Africa, and theoretically into psychological anthropology, acculturation studies, and peasant studies. Methodologically too, American anthropologists experimented with new systems, coded data retrieval, and controlled comparisons. British anthropologists were less experimental but some turned toward environmental and economic studies while others urged the addition of the historical dimension.

AMERICAN ECLECTICISM

Problems of juvenile delinquency, alienation, and general social change, especially subsequent to World War I, tended to focus public and academic interest on the individual and the various schools of psychology. Psychologists' attention was almost entirely directed toward studies within Western society. It remained for anthropologists to apply psychology cross culturally.

Culture and Personality

In America in the late 20s and 30s, a number of prominent Boasians became interested in the application and testing of psychological theory and method cross culturally. In the early years this work was known as culture and personality studies but the people involved in later research began to call the subdivision *psychological anthropology*. Culture and personality research involved the application of learning and Gestalt psychology and some Freudian theory to non-Western societies with a focus on the impact of culture on individuals. Some researchers looked to see how differing ideal adult personalities arose, while others were interested in culturally produced sexual differences.

Students today probably associate Edward Sapir (1884–1934) with the linguistic theory he developed with Benjamin Lee Whorf. The theory, known as the Whorf-Sapir hypothesis, states that language is not only a means of communication, but actually shapes perception and exemplifies each society's unique model of the world. Best known for work in linguistics, Sapir was also interested in the formation of personality. Though he did no field research in personality himself, through his writing and seminars he was instrumental in arousing interest in others.

He rejected the usual ethnographic description as an incomplete statement about the individual because it did not take into account variation or emotion. He proposed the application of psychological theory and technique cross culturally to remedy this fault. He said that cultural phenomena may be examined through two points of departure: for either psychological or cultural content. However, he felt that the true locus of culture was in the interactions of individuals and the meanings they abstracted for themselves as a result of their experiences. He was interested in the psychological reality of culture, the personal reality.

Sapir believed individuals learned many of their cultural patterns unconsciously just as they learned language patterns. Since the individual was the locus of culture, he suggested that some cultures would be easier on the individual; more harmonious and balanced thus offering greater opportunity for individual expression than others. Conversely, some cultures might be frustrating and disordered, producing misdirected effort and individual stress. In a somewhat strange use of terms, he called the first type *genuine culture*; the second, *spurious*. His interest in how culture affected the individual influenced Ruth Benedict and Margaret Mead in particular.

Ruth Fulton Benedict (1887–1948) came into anthropology rather late in life from a background of philosophy and literature. Her particular interest in personality and culture and psychological normality was stimulated by her association with Sapir and further encouraged by Boas, her professor. In an important study, "Anthropology and the Abnormal" (1934b), Benedict proposed the startling thesis that abnormality was culturally determined; that what was abnormal or "insane" in one society might be considered not only normal and sane, but perhaps even ideal in another. In other words, cultural sanity was not universal sanity and abnormal meant only that an individual did not behave according to the norms of his own culture.

Benedict pictured the individual at birth capable of being molded into a vast number of personality types, each society attempting to produce an ideal adult personality through the processes of enculturation. It was her thesis that from the great variation possible at birth, certain traits are considered socially desirable and they are inculcated in society's young. Thus, there is a push to conformity within a society but because of human plasticity, there is unlimited variety taking all possible societies into consideration.

Benedict pursued her interest in personality types largely depending upon field notes of her colleagues. (She did fieldwork but mostly in folklore and religion, not

Ruth Benedict, 1887–1948
*(Courtesy of New York Public
Library)*

in cross-cultural psychology.) She presented her conclusions in one of the best known of all anthropological books: *Patterns of Culture* (1934a). Studying several societies—Zuni, Dobu, and Kwakiutl—she tried to discover one master plan of psychological patterning for each society that accounted for its uniqueness. This was a configuration approach like Kroeber's, except that Benedict's identifying pattern was psychological, not stylistic. Drawing upon impressions from her own fieldwork at Zuni Pueblo, from Reo Fortune's ethnography of the Dobuans of Melanesia, and from Boas' notes on the Kwakiutl Indians of the Northwest Coast, she described the ideal personalities developed in each society. The Zuni she characterized as Apollonian: serene, peaceful, taking all things in moderation; the Dobuans she depicted as paranoid: suspicious, fearful, and immoderate; while the Kwakiutl appeared to her megalomaniac: self-centered, egotistic, and quick to feel slighted. Critics contended that her characterizations were exaggerated and that she ignored data that tended to disprove her thesis. Nevertheless, most agreed that some societies did seem to display a dominant personality type.

The possibility of infinite variation precluded high level generalization and causal explanation and Benedict's position has been considered the ultimate in cultural relativism. Typical of the Boasian particularistic approach, Benedict saw personality patterns as unique historical products. She did have a strong functional aspect to her work, for she saw culture as integrated and functioning to condition its members to the desired norms. However, she never clearly identified dependent and independent variables in her cultural configurations and never explained how they changed. Her emphasis was on the plasticity of personality and she took culture as fixed or given, never attempting to seek its cause.

Margaret Mead (1901–   ) was one of Benedict's students and her early work, including her doctoral dissertation, was in the culture and personality tradition of emphasis on the individual and the importance of the enculturation processes. Mead was especially interested in problems of adolescence—juvenile delinquency and general emotional disruption at puberty being a "hot" topic both among the scholars and general public in the 20s and 30s. There were those who thought it a biological given that at puberty, social and emotional disorders occurred, but others were equally convinced that those phenomena of adolescence were cultural and that assignment of such traits to "human nature" was merely overgeneralization from Western culture. Mead's early research was an attempt to separate biological from cultural inheritance. Her two books, *Growing up in New Guinea* (1930) and *Coming of Age in Samoa* (1928), dealt with the problem and she concluded that the emotional problems of adolescence were cultural.

Her next work, *Sex and Temperament* (1935), also dealt with biological versus cultural conditioning, this time in respect to male and female temperament. *Were there universal, biological masculine and feminine temperaments or were males and females culturally conditioned to norms of masculinity and femininity?* She sought to demonstrate that there were no universal temperament traits that were purely masculine or feminine; that masculinity or femininity expressed in personality was culturally created—for example, women are more passive than men, men are more aggressive. (Note that she is talking about temperament and personality, not reproductive functions or roles which anthropologists agreed might vary culturally—for example, in some societies men are potters, in others only women are.)

Mead saw the normal sex temperament as a product of enculturation but she had difficulty explaining the deviant individual. In *Sex and Temperament* (1935) for instance, she seems to imply that the deviant was the product of biology, not culture, and she never reconciled that conclusion with her position that temperament was culturally determined.

The criticism of Benedict's work was mild compared to that leveled on Mead's study of sex differences. R. Fortune (1939), an anthropologist who had lived with the Arapesh—a group in which, according to Mead, both men and women showed temperaments that we would call feminine—claimed that had Mead been allowed to join the all-male groups, she would never have characterized Arapesh men as she did. Mead, a woman, was prevented from seeing all aspects of the society because some activities were exclusively male. Other, harsher criticism suggested that the chance discovery of three societies that seemed to prove her contentions was just too good to be true and some wondered why no one else ever came upon such data. However, Mead's work was provocative and certainly, in light of the feminist movement of the 60s and 70s, in advance of its time. (She answered some of her critics in the preface to the 1950 edition of *Sex and Temperament*.)

As a result of years of research on the psychological patterning of Ojibwa Indians, A. I. Hallowell was able to connect variables of culture change and personal stress in situations of contact between the Ojibwa and Europeans. Studying three Ojibwa communities, each representing a different degree of acculturation, and using Rorschach and TAT protocols as well as historical data, Hallowell concluded that in many ways traditional Ojibwa personality characteristics persisted in spite of long term contact with a technologically dominant society. The same psychological traits that early European visitors had observed appeared to have endured in varying degrees through more than 200 years of contact and change in material culture. He found, furthermore, that erosion or regression had occurred in personality structures of some partly acculturated individuals as the old ways had been lost without suitable cultural substitutes replacing them.

National Character Studies

Before and during the Second World War, interdisciplinary groups of scholars, including anthropologists, joined with the federal government to conduct studies for psychological warfare. Benedict and Mead were prominently involved. Their association with the war effort was quite an about-face from the nonintervention stand of Boasians during World War I. The excesses of Hitlerian Germany united anthropologists as well as other behavioral scientists in backing government research in psychological warfare. That research became known as *National Character Studies*.

Such studies could not be conducted in the field because of the obvious impossibility of fieldwork in an enemy nation. The participants, therefore, had to develop a new methodology for gaining psychological insights. They made their studies using many sources—anything, in fact, except fieldwork. They did analyses of literature, films, news media, and conducted interviews of prisoners of war and expatriates. Because of the absence of fieldwork, the method is often referred to as the study of *culture at a distance*. The most famous publication resulting from this research was Benedict's study of Japanese character, *The Chrysanthemum and the Sword* (1946), which was acknowledged as a major effort but also criticized by many for its dependence on data solely from the upper-middle class, for ignoring class distinctions and associated behavior, and for overlooking cultural change, thus producing a static typology.

Attempts at describing complex societies have continued but they diminished after the 50s. Difficulties of the sort exposed by the criticisms of Benedict's work have been almost insurmountable in view of the many variables in multi-class and multi-ethnic societies.

Freudian Approaches

In the early years, although culture and personality studies derived adult personality types on the basis of childhood socialization, they leaned heavily on learning theory, Watson's behavior theory, Gestalt psychology, and general child psychology, and had little Freudian content. Briefly, Freudian theory says that certain psychological characteristics and responses are innate, permanent, and universal; that there are psychological mechanisms, capacities, and symbolism common to all human beings. That is, Freudian theory predicated universal unconscious forces within the personality: the id—repressed impulses or instinctual drives of the unconscious self; the super-ego—individual conscience or awareness of culturally derived values that restrict the id; and the ego—the conscious self that mediates between the id and the super-ego. The theory also suggests that certain psychological mechanisms like repression, projection, and sublimation are universal. Whereas Mead, Benedict, and their followers attempted to demonstrate the impact of culture on behavior, the Freudians have looked for behavior arising from universal human endowment in psychological structures and they believe that character is formed as a child is required to cope with those structures during the socialization process.

For many years, anthropologists resisted application of Freud's psychoanalytic theories—derived from nineteenth century Viennese patients—to native societies and most anthropologists dismissed Freud's interpretation of anthropological materials in his book, *Totem and Taboo* (1938). Malinowski, as mentioned, believed that he had demonstrated that the Oedipus complex in its classical form was not universal, but another researcher, Geza Roheim, who was psychoanalytically trained, thought that Malinowski was wrong. Roheim believed that in a wider sense, Freud's contentions held true and somewhat facetiously suggested that those who resisted a Freudian interpretation were in the clutches of their own Oedipal complexes.

Analysis of the basic personality structure of society was a method developed by psychoanalyst Abram Kardiner in cooperation with anthropologists Ralph Linton and Cora DuBois. Abram Kardiner represents a serious and meticulous researcher who tried to apply Freudian theory to anthropology and hoped to produce psychological characterizations of culture. From ethnographic data, he tried to infer the basic personality of a society—the pattern shared by the majority of the people as a result of their common childhood socialization process. The anthropologists checked Kardiner's results with projective tests done in the field as well as with their own interpretations of the adult personality of the people. An important study was conducted on a Pacific Island people, the Alorese, by Cora DuBois.

Kardiner thought that by knowing the child-rearing practices (which he called the primary institutions) and the secondary institutions (government, religion, myth, and so on), inferences could be made about the basic personality of an individual. A specialist, Emil Oberholzer, interpreted the projective tests—Rorschach Ink-Blot Tests—given the Alorese. All participants in analysis worked "blind"; that is, no one knew any other's findings. Good correspondence between the conclusions of the psychologists and the anthropologists was obtained although there were questions left unanswered about the use of projective tests cross culturally.

The theory behind all projective tests—Rorschachs, TATs (thematic apperception tests), and so on—is that anyone projects his inner sentiments and attitudes into his interpretation of the tests and expresses those inner states in fantasy. Thus, general motivational tendencies may be discerned in his fictional description of what he perceives. The use of projective tests reached a peak in the 50s and then diminished. Most researchers believe that carefully controlled, the tests can answer such questions as: what is the most frequent response within a society?; what is typical and what is deviant?; and how variable are the personalities within one culture? However, much more testing must be done cross culturally before meaningful comparative statements can be made.

Using ethnographic material already available rather than doing fieldwork, John Whiting and Irvin Child of Yale University tried to test some hypotheses incorporating Freudian theory and personality development. They used data from the Human Relations Area Files (which will be discussed later) to test their hypothesis that infant and childhood indulgence in one of the five primary systems of behavior (oral, anal, sexual, dependence, and aggression) would increase satisfaction in that system in adulthood, whereas early punishment would increase the likelihood of anxiety and conflict in that system later in life. They meant, for example, that any child fed at request would seek and receive oral gratification of some sort in adulthood, but a child whose food was served very irregularly would tend to develop anxieties about food and general oral responses later on in life.

After making appropriate statistical studies from the Human Relations Area Files, Whiting and Child concluded that the positive case was not proved but that the negative was generally substantiated. The most conclusive evidence for negative fixation (the negative case) came from the oral, dependence, and aggression systems which suggested that Freudian theory exaggerated the strength of the anal and sexual drives.

Statistical Cross-cultural Comparisons

Whiting and Child did their hypothesis testing by using a coded data retrieval system originated by George Peter Murdock and his colleagues at Yale University. Murdock was outside the Boasian stream of anthropology having studied under sociologist Albert Keller at Yale and he set an early goal of developing a field theory approach to social science that would include social anthropology (he paid little attention to physical anthropology and archaeology), psychology, and sociology. In his early career, he referred to himself as a professor of the Science of Society but under influence from Wissler and Sapir he turned more to social anthropology and took a position as Professor of Anthropology at Yale. He was convinced that social anthropology and sociology should really be a single discipline and that its proper subject matter was cultural behavior, independent of biology.

Murdock felt strongly that whatever Boas' reasons for avoiding generalization and cross-cultural comparisons early in the century, by mid-century there were already gathered adequate data to test hypotheses; in other words, there should be a return to theory building. He turned to ethnographic studies and using categories similar to those suggested by Wissler as universals of culture compiled the cross-cultural survey, called the Human Relations Area Files after 1949. The files would make available ethnographic data that could be used for testing hypotheses without the need for fieldwork. In a form that lent itself to statistical correlations, the files made possible sampling techniques to demonstrate "adhesions" of the sort Tylor had proposed in the nineteenth century but the data were very much better. The HRAF (as the files are abbreviated) were established at Yale and in a few decades at universities in all regions of the United States and in many foreign countries though the English universities remained indifferent to the idea.

Murdock demonstrated the use of the files in research for his most important book, *Social Structure* (1949), in which he focused on the topics of family and kinship organization in societies indexed in the files. He compiled correlations and generalized in "an insignificant fraction of the time required for comparable library research."

Benefits of any coded, cross indexed data retrieval system are the sheer volume of information and the greater speed of recovery. However, as critics have pointed out, there are also a number of problems that must be taken into consideration as one uses the files for the extraction of ethnographic variables. Some of the more serious are: uneven, questionable, or inadequate coverage in the literature that is indexed; aspects of culture ripped from context; and the question of independence of cases—that is, does one count each case separately even though all may be derived from a single source? How can anyone be sure there is control for diffusion? In addition, any researcher using the files must make many subjective judgments. For example, how much importance should be attached to an ethnographer's unquantified statements of presence of a trait—is it rare, occasional, or widespread through a society? Far too often, it is not at all clear.

Limited Comparison

Another American to break away from the Boasian strictures against generalization and comparison was Fred Eggan who, stimulated by Radcliffe-Brown's stay at the University of Chicago, attempted a combination of structural-functional and diachronic analysis. Eggan proposed a method of controlled comparison on a small scale in a direction quite unlike Murdock's. He put the idea of limited comparison to work in his study of the western Pueblo (a single structural type with good archaeological and historical records) to analyze the variation and its cause found among the different groups. By using controlled situations, Eggan believed it possible to work out the processes by which structural change occurred and to test hypotheses in comparative perspective.

The Folk-Urban Continuum

Standing somewhat outside the Boas circle but closely associated with some of its members, Robert Redfield began the study of peasant or folk societies in the 30s. He was influenced by sociologists Robert Park and Louis Wirth and by Durkheim's concept of societal development by division of labor. He also found useful the distinction between *Gemeinschaft* and *Gesellschaft* (community and society) applied by Ferdinand Tönnies to the study of change from feudal to capitalist society. From these Redfield developed an evolutionary sequence—the folk-urban continuum. Unlike the sequences of the classical evolutionists, Redfield's developmental scheme was in ideal types as points along a continuum of change, not as stages or levels. The rural or folk extreme is small, isolated, and homogeneous, characterized by strong religious beliefs and intimate face-to-face relationships; while the urban pole is secular, heterogeneous, and impersonal. The folk society is integrated by its tightly knit kinship structures, common sentiments, and shared values; the urban society by its functional complementarity. This continuum applies not only to change from country to city but also corresponds to prehistoric human development from small community to civilizations resulting from the agricultural-urban revolution.

Redfield saw ideas as a major force in change and he is usually classified as a cultural idealist—one who sees culture in terms of common beliefs and shared norms. Redfield's definition of culture is "common understandings manifest in art and artifact" and he pictured the ethnographer's job as trying to comprehend those common understandings.

His fieldwork was among peasant or folk societies and his strong support for the idealist view of culture led him to look for the goals and system of ideas held by the members of society rather than at the actual behavior manifestations of the people. His study of a Mexican town, Tepoztlan, became the object of a classical debate when, 20 years later, Oscar Lewis did a restudy of the town and came up with almost diametrically opposed conclusions. The difference between the results of the two men's work seems to lie in their orientations. (The time lapse was considered unimportant in this case.) Redfield had recorded the normative culture while Lewis described the behavior of the people. Redfield's ethnography painted Tepoztlan as harmonious and serene, personally satisfying. Lewis detailed angry factionalism, drunken brawling, and many barely concealed antagonisms in personal relationships. Those two studies depict as nothing else can how the predilections, theoretical positions, and biases of ethnographers can affect research.

Acculturation Studies

By the 30s, the American anthropologists had begun working in Oceania and Africa, and Melville Herskovits established the first African Studies Program in the United States at Northwestern University. But whether in one area of the world or another, a paramount interest of the Boasians was change and cultural dynamics. Their historical focus predisposed them to the study of culture change but perhaps more importantly the problems of change, social dislocation, and social disorientation had become apparent among American Indian societies and the underdeveloped and colonial nations of the world. This in turn directed the interest of social scientists toward processes of change. Studies under conditions of long-term contact between two societies and the ensuing changes in either or both groups became popular among American anthropologists, though the English were never much attracted.

The term *acculturation* was not new—it had been used occasionally in the nineteenth century to mean accommodation and change by which two cultures became more alike. However, the increased use in the mid-twentieth century required more precise definition and in "Memorandum on the Study of Acculturation" (1936) by Robert Redfield, Ralph Linton, and Melville Herskovits, acculturation was defined as "those phenomena which result when groups of individuals having different cultures come into continuous first-hand contact, with subsequent changes in the original cultural patterns of both groups." This discriminated between acculturation and other forms of culture change. In keeping with Boas' warning against premature theorizing, most acculturation studies fell within the historical particularistic mold but some generalization did result.

Acculturation studies attempted to be studies of change in process. Methodologically, they required a base-line condition from which change was measured. The base-line situation could be reconstructed through techniques of ethnohistory, using any written materials, folklore, and interviews. That was followed by description and analysis of change. There was a practical element to the studies since they carried an implication for applied anthropology and administration in colonial territories or on Indian reservations or even within the dominant American society among immigrant and ethnic groups and for social welfare programs in cities. Though theoretically the studies could be made on contact situations between two non-Western societies, in fact, virtually all were between a native group and an industrial, western group and only rarely did they actually deal with the two-way nature of change, usually examining change only as it affected the non-European society.

Some specific points of research were: the means of introducing change; the degree of resistance to change; the mechanisms of selection; changes in roles and statuses; and final products of change like assimilation, reinterpretation, syncretism, and revitalization. All this interest in cultural processes indicated a new impulse among Boasians to generalize about cause and effect and to make cross-cultural comparisons about the mechanisms or common properties of changing cultural systems.

Configuration Theory

To some degree in response to British functionalism and in some degree to bring coherence and order to the breadth of information being collected under the heading of culture, Kroeber and Benedict had contrived the idea of pattern or configuration— the cluster of characteristics that identified or sorted out specific societies. Benedict's configuration was the typical personality of adults; Kroeber used styles and major motifs to identify societies. In the middle years of the twentieth century, other anthropologists attempted the characterization of typology of societies by their dominant attributes. Philosopher David Bidney, who became interested in anthropological theory, suggested the use of philosophical postulates under which each cultural system operated as the focal points of identifying characteristics.

Another philosophical approach was taken by Florence Kluckhohn and Fred Strodtbeck in *Variations in Value Orientations* (1961), in which they both suggested that people as a group could be characterized by their basic orientation among trichotomies or three part categories—for example, focus on the past, present, or future. They proposed classification weighted according to the cultural emphasis in various values as plausible means of typing societies. Clyde Kluckhohn proposed identification by choice between binary categories, the relative emphasis societies placed on opposites—good, bad; individual, group and so on. Kluckhohn also said that each society worked on basic premises which he called the "givens" of society. From those basic premises, proper and improper behavior could be defined. He applied "givens" to the Navajo to describe their society.

Probably the most detailed were the *themes* conceived by Morris Opler in "Themes as Dynamic Forces in Culture" (1945) and "Component, Assemblage, and Theme in Cultural Integration and Differentiation" (1959). He described his themes as "dynamic affirmations"—values that controlled behavior or stimulated activity—that show up in behavior. For instance, if a theme is that men are superior to women, it will be translated into conduct in the order in which men and women walk, eat, and participate in rituals. However, he proposed there are always "counterthemes" that provided balance. Women are highly valued in certain sectors of activity: horticulture, child rearing, and so on.

Critics of configurationism pointed out the weaknesses: the characterizations are too simplistic and tend to be caricatures. The descriptions are too idiosyncratic;

different observers see different patterns. All attempts to develop configurations are descriptions and explain nothing. The British social anthropologists found no merit in typing or characterizing cultures and in fact configuration approaches have become unpopular because of the conceptual and operational problems.

BRITISH ANTHROPOLOGY IN MID-CENTURY

In this period, social anthropology showed much theoretical and substantive continuity with the earlier years of the century. The British continued to avoid the breadth and most of the innovations attracting the Americans during these decades. The British Empire, rapidly becoming their former empire after World War II, persisted as focus of field research and the structural-functional orientation was the theoretical viewpoint. However, a few of the students of both Malinowski and Radcliffe-Brown perceived a need for the addition of the time dimension to their studies as change became the most obvious fact about native societies, and some scholars developed an interest in environment and economics.

Adding Historical Depth

Edward Evan Evans-Pritchard (1902–1973) and Edmund Leach (1910–   ) stand out for their belief that historical factors could no longer be ignored, though their approaches were in no way similar. Evans-Pritchard, who had studied under Malinowski and succeeded Radcliffe-Brown at Oxford, came to the conclusion after extensive fieldwork in Africa that historical perspective was necessary for the real understanding of societies. The change wrought by European contact was of such magnitude that traditional structural-functionalism had become inadequate. In fact, Evans-Pritchard came to think of anthropology as a kind of historiography and therefore as a discipline properly belonging in the humanities, not in the sciences. Alone among the British, he took the position that social systems are moral systems, not natural systems; that anthropology should seek patterns, not scientific laws, and should interpret rather than explain.

In his Marett Lecture (reprinted in Evans-Pritchard, 1964) he made a public commitment to his humanistic stand. He elaborated the theoretical position expressed in that essay in another, "Anthropology and History," suggesting that anthropologists and historians alike see the general in the particular and that anthropologists should begin to treat historical materials sociologically, carefully using the oral traditions of nonliterate peoples, a proposal not unlike the approaches of American culture historians.

Evans-Pritchard's work on Nuer religion (1956) was in marked contrast to Durkheim's theory that religion was in the final analysis society worshipping itself. Evans-Pritchard saw religion as a legitimate form of explanation of the mysteries of the world and he tried to present a coherent picture of the Nuer conception of spirit and man's relations to it. He suggested that the only way to understand religion is to understand what it means to the believers themselves. Though clearly a functionalist, Evans-Pritchard urged investigation of the more subjective aspects of culture—the view from inside the structure. His position thus became a major departure from the structural-functionalism of Radcliffe-Brown.

Edmund Leach, a student of Malinowski, was similarly impressed with the need for time depth as a result of his field experience in Burma during World War II. He found that the political situation of tribal societies he was studying was inexplicable by synchronic functional analysis and he wrote *Political Systems of Highland Burma* (1954), a study of political change that was in essence a severe critique of the structural-functional model of closed, static systems. He insisted that the typology of fixed systems so popular with his colleagues had little correspondence to reality and that no synchronic study could be an accurate description because societies did not show tendencies toward stability or equilibrium. Leach felt that British social anthropologists had made a serious error in their emphasis on integration and social solidarity because such a theoretical stance blinded them to conflict, stress, and change. Real societies can never be in equilibrium. He believed that the stable, structural view of society was nothing more than the ethnographer imposing personally conceptualized categories on native lifeways. Whatever benefits had once been derived from structural-functional analysis, it had lost its freshness and flexibility by midcentury. A new model was needed and it had to include historical dimensions. Leach stressed the need for understanding behavior on three levels: the actual, observable behavior of members of society; the average (or norm) of all the actual behaviors; and the peoples' own description of their behavior, or the ideal. (Leach's later work will be discussed in the next chapter.)

Max Gluckman (1911–1975) represents another position. Continuing to operate within the tradition of his teacher, Radcliffe-Brown, Gluckman supported the notion of equilibrium in society. Gluckman's special interests were political organization and judicial processes and his contribution was in theory of conflict and equilibrium within the structuralist-functional orientation. He posited that conflicts are always present among the elements of social structure, but that within the wider context, conflicts are resolved before the social system is destroyed. For example, even though groups may be in opposition, at least some of their members some of the time must act together in matters affecting society. Therefore, the forces tending toward fission are always more or less kept in balance with those of fusion through reciprocal obligations. The same element or custom may at once be divisive and also cohesive—like witchcraft—which may be disruptive but also operates as a means of social control. The tradition of social solidarity through complementarity and functional interrelatedness of social elements can be traced back from Gluckman through Radcliffe-Brown to Durkheim.

In the 50s as the colonial empire broke apart, critics like Leach assailed Gluckman's model as too static to deal with social change and further criticized it for forcing facts into preconceived categories. Though Gluckman denied that his strategy was inadequate for the study of social change, he did make some modification through the addition of historical development to help understand the present structure. His inclusion of time depth did not mean abandoning the idea of equilibrium. Instead, he looked to see how disturbances were followed by recovery of balance—equilibrium through time. He concluded that present structures encapsulate everything structurally relevant in their past phases but that they may not include the same personnel or combinations in the same proportions. Gluckman also turned from Radcliffe-Brown's organic analogy because he concluded that social systems were not really comparable to organic systems—not so integrated or repetitive.

Gluckman took a look at colonialism in a broader perspective. As the Director of the Rhodes-Livingstone Institute, he had plans to study the interrelations among tribal peoples, colonial administrations, merchants, and settlers (both European and Asian)—a study in the context of a plural society. He was also interested in comparing precolonial and colonial structures but he left the Institute for a professorship in England before all these plans were realized. Known as the developer of the department at the University of Manchester, Gluckman trained many younger British anthropologists with a strong focus on studies of the processes of conflict and conflict resolution.

Environment and Economy

C. D. Forde's *Habitat, Economy, and Society* (1934) represented something new in British social anthropology. It was a forerunner of what in America later became a major theoretical stance: *cultural ecology*, although Forde referred to his work as *human geography*. In this book, Forde made an attempt to break out of the closed system model of the structural-functionalists with the inclusion of environment and technology or economy as influential factors, if not exactly causal or determinative ones and by considering the relation of economy to environment, social organization, and major factors in the growth of civilization. Forde's work may be an example of the cross-fertilization between American and British anthropologists, for he visited the United States and acknowledged as intellectually stimulating the ideas generated by Wissler and Kroeber who were engaged in refining the culture area concept.

From his studies on societies of various degrees of complexity, Forde drew some generalizations: hunting and gathering peoples were ancestral to all mankind but pure collectors, like those posited by Morgan, are ethnographically unknown. All human groups regardless of sociocultural complexity have some concept of territoriality and political complexity is positively correlated with economic complexity, the range of variation among cultivators being greater than among hunters and gatherers. Women are the cultivators in middle-range societies practicing hand-tool cultivation and plough agriculture is associated with male cultivators. Some of these generalizations had been made in the nineteenth century by the evolutionists and some seem almost too obvious to mention, but Forde's conclusions were based on solid ethnographic evidence, not speculation.

Economic Anthropology

Raymond Firth, well known as the ethnographer of the Tikopia, is probably even more renowned for his application of economic theory to anthropology. He became interested in primitive economics because in his fieldwork he saw how many social relationships were made apparent by their economic content. He urged more studies combining and correlating economy, ecology, and environment with social structure.

Firth, a student of Malinowski, was greatly impressed by the Kula ring exchange system and he thought that he could apply formal economic theory of industrial society to analysis of primitive society. Substantivists, those who deny that formal economic theory is applicable to primitive economics, have vigorously opposed Firth's position. They claim that formal theory is too culture-bound. Continuing debate between the formalists and substantivists has characterized economic anthropology and Firth continues to maintain his theoretical position formulated over 30 years ago. Across the Atlantic, Melville Herskovits, Paul J. Bohannan, and George Dalton entered into the substantivist-formalist controversy, all taking—in varying degrees—a substantivist position.

Firth also felt that the synchronic approach needed revising. For greater clarity, he found it advisable to make a distinction between social organization and social structure. Social structure is the abstract, formal ideal and norm, but it rarely occurs in fact. Ongoing social interactions and relationships, therefore, need another classification which he has called *social organization*. It is in social organization that people exercise choices and make decisions while the social structure is a relatively unchanging set of principles and an analytic construct. Social structure is static; social organization is dynamic. In separating structure from organization, Firth was trying to overcome the problem of change inherent in Radcliffe-Brown's model. Eventually, patterned and repeated change in organization will be reflected in an altered structure.

Evolutionism in British Archaeology

In Britain as in America, evolutionist theories had fallen into disfavor under attack from social and cultural anthropologists. However, V. Gordon Childe (1892–1957), an Australian and probably *the* outstanding British archaeologist of the twentieth century, revived social evolutionism and combined it with diffusion in his reconstruction of European prehistory. At a time when virtually all other anthropologists repudiated cultural evolution as an unacceptable theoretical stance, Childe found the concept helpful in understanding the development and spread of social complexity from southwest Asia into Europe in prehistoric times.

In his early work, Childe merely elaborated on the Three Age concept: stone, bronze, and iron, dividing the Paleolithic from the Neolithic not on the old criterion of stone tool manufacturing techniques, but redefining the Neolithic as the beginning of food production based on domestication of plants and animals and the appearance of village life. His interpretation endowed the category with more socioeconomic content than was customary in archaeological studies. He replaced simplistic Victorian successions with complex cultural interaction between invention and diffusion and made limited, careful interpretation of non-material culture from material remains. He viewed the periods as having the same basic socioeconomic content wherever they occurred but pointed out that they were not coincidental in absolute time around the world.

Then Childe visited Russia in the 30s and was impressed with the Russian application of Morgan's work. He began to use Morgan's classifications—*savagery*, *barbarism*, and *civilization*—in his own work, equating the Paleolithic and Mesolithic with savagery; Neolithic with barbarism; and the development of cities, which he called the Urban Revolution, with the beginning of civilization. From their geographic origins, he traced the diffusion of traits and ideas to outlying areas, continuing his orientation toward the combination of diffusion and migration with evolution.

Childe also gave a definition or characterization of civilization that has become commonly accepted in anthropology: "aggregation of large populations in cities; the differentiation within these of primary producers . . . full-time specialist artisans, merchants, officials, priests, and rulers; an effective concentration of economic and political power; the use of conventional symbols for recording and transmitting information (writing); and equally conventional standards of weights and of measures of time and space leading to some mathematical and calendrical science." (Childe 1963: 158)

CULTURAL (AMERICAN) AND SOCIAL (BRITISH) ANTHROPOLOGY

American and British cultural and social approaches to anthropology are more alike than unlike and visiting professors from each side of the Atlantic have tended to take on the characteristics of their temporary colleagues. The two orientations have enriched each other. American students of anthropology today probably read far more contemporary British anthropology than classical American works of Boas, Lowie, or Kroeber. Yet there are some real differences between anthropology in the two countries today as well as differences in historical development.

American Anthropology

In many ways, American anthropology was shaped by the fact of there being New World natives right in the backyard, so to speak. American Indians had been a matter of curiosity to Europeans from the time of first contact and had intrigued professional anthropologists as well as dabblers and dilettantes. The question of Indian origins was paramount and that interest as well as Indian migrations and changes after European contact guaranteed an historical slant to American ethnology. To be interested in Indians was to be interested in history and prehistory. In addition, Boas' early association with the study of geography and the influence of Dilthey predisposed him toward research in space-time studies and he in turn instilled this orientation in his students.

American Indians had suffered and were suffering deprivation and oppression at the time anthropology in America was becoming professionalized. It took no great thought to realize that Indian societies, once secure and powerful, were socially disorganized and in danger of total destruction. Many concerned persons—among them anthropologists—wished not only to alleviate the suffering but also to capture everything possible of past Indian life and traditions before they disappeared entirely. This desire resulted in attempts at reconstructing aboriginal cultures through techniques of ethnohistory: interviews with elders, use of whatever documentation was pertinent or available in the form of old letters, journals, diaries, and archaeological information, and interpretations of legends. Even linguistic connections were pertinent in establishing culture change and migrations. Thus, American Indian studies added an orientation toward both time depth and broad coverage.

In addition, the burgeoning populations and growth of universities and colleges in America meant that there were increasingly more job openings in anthropology. The relatively open market for university professors tended to put a premium on innovation and originality in American scholarship. Rather than replicate, reconfirm, or revise older research, American university students sought to do something new: study groups never before recorded, research new problems, and experiment with new techniques. There was little reason to confine research in any way—another impetus to the great variety that has become typical of American anthropology.

American anthropology developed into a discipline that is holistic or extensive, including physical anthropology, ethnology, archaeology, and linguistics, unified by the concept of culture, and very tolerant of innovation in methodology or content. It arose in a period of intellectual and liberal concern for minorities and oppressed groups and many professionals have been actively involved with social welfare at home and in the developing nations of the world.

British Anthropology

Social anthropology as it developed in Britain was both more restricted and more intensive than American cultural anthropology which tended toward holism and extensiveness. The British, except Malinowski, found culture an unwieldy concept—"too much reality"—and preferred to focus on relatively stable roles, relationships, and social groups. Therefore, British anthropology is often considered synonymous with "social" anthropology.

The needs of the Empire were served by this orientation—though not usually deliberately or even consciously. But British social anthropologists were as much a part of their social matrix as any native of his and the Empire was the ground of their fieldwork. Unlike the New World natives, the natives of the British colonies were not disappearing; they were often increasing and always the need to keep them under control was in the minds of colonial government officials. This government orientation fit in well with the developing interests of the anthropologists themselves in social organization—how native groups organized and what held them together. It has also been charged that the colonial situation was conducive to seeing native social systems as static and that the anthropologists' synchronic, functionalist approach lent itself particularly well to this view.

The academic traditions in Britain were restrictive also. Compared to the numbers of institutions of higher learning opening and expanding in the United States, university positions in Britain were limited indeed and the academic ladder differed too. Professors were not added to the staff in most British universities until the older members retired and those older members were often instrumental in choosing their replacements. Consequently, young British academicians, having to please those in power, tended not to wander far afield into new research areas. In America, innovation, originality, experimentation, and variety became the means to success; in England, reworking old problems and investigating old theories in greater detail were the way to professional achievement and recognition.

The needs of the government reinforced anthropological interest in social groups and the limited job opportunities and need to please elder academicians tended to prevent investigation in new areas. As a result, the British became justifiably known for their superb and thorough studies of kinship and research on social organization. They largely ignored cultural history, cross-cultural study of psychology, and most of the other areas typical of the expanding American anthropology. In addition, departments of anthropology in British schools did not include physical anthropology and archaeology which were situated in other departments like biology or classics, or were departments in their own right.

6

Current Anthropology, 1960–

In the 60s, depersonalization and the predicament of the isolated individual in unfriendly and unfeeling society became a topic in literature and art as well as in the behavioral sciences. Things and events often seemed beyond human control. Increasing emphasis on subjective analysis and personal experience as well as reactions of individuals against society or the establishment characterized the decade. Skepticism, cynicism, disillusion with authority, and opposition to government policy in the Vietnam conflict combined with racial strife and deteriorating conditions in cities and led to intellectual alienation and withdrawal from civic participation by many young adults. Common feelings of personal helplessness in the face of social forces beyond individual control turned people to greater introspection, and dissent was often marked by "dropping out" or "turning off" as popular speech put it.

Contradictions in American democratic theory and practice at home and the war in southeast Asia caused a reappraisal of American policy by students, minorities, and many others. Some saw America as a colonial power with a history of slavery and Indian persecution. In addition, concern over technology and its probable destructive consequences on environment arose. Assumptions about an uninvolved science came under question. Under question also was the anthropological assumption that nontechnological societies wanted to remain that way—especially in view of their proclaimed drives toward technological modernization. The Third World nations rejected their position as traditional societies and strove to enter the cosmopolitan world culture.

The increasing subjectiveness and interest in the individual were reflected in the renewed interest on the part of some anthropologists in seeing and recording culture as viewed strictly by the culture-bearers. This attempt at an orientation from the inside produced a major effort to clarify and discriminate between the analytic and the native points of view. Though many anthropologists had recognized the essential conflict between the two orientations and the need to separate the two (some of the more notable anthropologists were: Firth in his attempt to separate social structure and social organization, Redfield and Lewis in their treatment and conclusions about Tepoztlan, and Leach in his separation of norms and ideals of behavior), confusion between the two viewpoints—the analytic and the folk—continued to be a problem because so few ethnographers clearly distinguished them in their work.

The terms *etic* and *emic*, derived from the words *phonetic* and *phonemic*, were introduced and became popular in anthropological literature. Etic, from phonetic (a standardized system of recording voice communication understandable to anyone trained in its use), signifies a scientific judgment that can be verified by any other trained observer. An emic point of view (from phoneme, a sound unit meaningful only to speakers of a particular language) is one from within a particular culture—the view of the culture actor in terms of his conceptual categories.

COGNITIVE ANTHROPOLOGY

The usage of the term *cognitive anthropology* has not yet been standardized but it appears to be used with increasing frequency to include the subcategories of ethnoscience and symbolic anthropology, though some would consider the latter a separate domain entirely. As the term suggests, there is a strong emphasis on cognition, and while the contents have not yet been universally agreed upon or conventionalized, we include here the categories mentioned above as well as the mazeway formulation of Anthony Wallace.

It is plausible to see the roots of cognitive anthropology in the work of Edward Sapir, who stated decades earlier that cultural behavior is symbolic behavior shared by the culture bearers and cultures are abstractions of ideas and behavior patterns with different meanings for different individuals. The anthropologist should describe the abstracted patterns and derive the various meanings from the particular people studied and not use his own categories. This attempt to understand native categories is what is implied by cognitive anthropology. It is an effort to get at the organizing principles that underlie behavior within each society.

A movement called *ethnoscience* or the *New Ethnography*, already suggested in the 50s, achieved wider attention and expressed the anthropological interest in a mentalist approach. In itself, the attempt to get the native view was not new; Boas had said a culture should be studied in its own terms and Malinowski stated that the ethnographer must grasp the native's view. What was new was the effort to eliminate the ethnographer's categories entirely.

Popular recognition of ethnoscience can be traced to Ward Goodenough, particularly to his 1956 article, "Componential Analysis." While ethnoscience is basically a methodology—hence the alternate name, New Ethnography—it has a theoretical underpinning: real culture exists only in the minds of the culture bearers. Each native of a society has his own mental template or map of the culture, which is, as Goodenough put it, what the individual must know to operate successfully within his society. Because it is so totally individualistic and mentalistic, ethnoscience has unkindly been called the last gasp of cultural relativism.

The people who advanced ethnoscience were seeking a way of eliciting information without placing that information in the preconceived categories of the ethnographer. To avoid imposing his own classifications, the ethnoscientist turned to linguistic procedures using only the native language to get the informants' own classification. The final product, if the procedures are properly followed, is a taxonomy perhaps, or a model of all components germane to the universe of enquiry completely free of the ethnographer's cultural categories. Most ethnoscience research so far has dealt with restricted domains like folk medicine, color categories, and plant classification. It is a time-consuming technique and complete recovery of just one individual's total perceptions would take at least a lifetime.

Many critics of ethnoscience have expressed their opposition but perhaps most of them have missed or ignored the point that those involved have never advocated abandoning more traditional methodology. They have suggested the New Ethnography as an additional means of data gathering. Detractors, however, have been skeptical that anyone can get inside another's head to know what he really thinks and how he really perceives. Furthermore, behaviorists really do not care whether it is possible because they are interested only in what people do, not what they think. Another criticism is that though ethnoscience may be interesting, there is no indication that it can be useful. It is too individualistic and relativistic for comparison, quantification, or establishing generalizations—goals most anthropologists consider the whole point of research to be. Nevertheless, some ethnoscientists believe that there may be a universal, basic structure to organizing principles and human systems of classification and that it may eventually be discerned through the methodology of ethnoscience.

Anthony Wallace took another approach to cognitive studies. Noting that all individuals classify or organize experience in some meaningful way, he developed the concept of the *mazeway*—the individual's own cognitive map of social roles and appropriate cultural behavior. Wallace says that one person's mazeway need not duplicate any other's in a society but only overlap enough in those areas important to mutual expectations to allow accurate predictions. He points out that no single individual commands total knowledge of his society and therefore needs other members to complement him. Thus, Wallace postulates that cognitive variability rather than cognitive consonance characterizes society. Under conditions of rapid culture change, the mazeway may break down and require reordering into a new state. If reordering of the traditional modes does not, or cannot occur, individuals cannot function. If the resynthesis of the mazeway is successful, the individual has a new guide to behavior within his changed social milieu.

What has been called *symbolic anthropology* represents another cognitive or mentalist orientation. It may be seen as a sophisticated extension of the concept of culture and culture patterning or as another approach within the broader functionalist tradition (for example, symbolic systems have maintenance functions or psychological functions). Prominent among those associated with symbolic anthropology are Clifford Geertz, David Schneider, Victor Turner, and Mary Douglas. These people have in common a view of culture as a symbolic system, though their points of departure vary.

David Schneider, for example, has focused on American kinship as a system of symbols—a system treated in its own terms and not related to social, biological, or psychological systems. This means that the biological facts of kinship represent something more than the facts themselves; they symbolize qualities like enduring solidarity and trust.

Clifford Geertz has suggested that through symbols, people define their world and also transform it into their model of the universe. He describes religion as a symbolic system that reinforces the nature of the real world for the people and also reinforces the emotions with which humans perceive the real world. That is, it symbolizes and interprets human existence and also the reasons for human existence, the nature of life, and the worldview of the people.

Victor Turner, a student of Max Gluckman, turned his attention toward religion and ritual. He has analyzed ritual symbols in Ndembu society as factors in social action. He believes that symbols must be studied within a particular cultural context and his work is carefully empirical, based on fieldwork aimed at understanding what the symbols mean to the members of the society. However, he believes that gathering *emic* data alone is not enough; he thinks *etic* descriptions and analyses are equally important.

Mary Douglas has taken a different approach to the study of symbols. She has attempted to find universal symbols: those symbols which have appeared in many periods and cultures. The work on primitive classification done by Durkheim and Mauss stimulated Douglas' research. She assumes that the symbolic order in some way reflects the social order and she has hypothesized that one might seek what she calls natural symbols by looking at the ways in which the images of the human body have been used cross culturally.

French Structuralism

Another recent approach that concerns itself with psychology in the sense that it deals with cognitive processes has been French structuralism, pioneered by Claude Levi-Strauss. It began some years before the 60s, but Levi-Strauss' ideas and research did not catch on in America and England until that decade. The word *structuralism* applied to Levi-Strauss 'and his colleagues in anthropology and to structuralists in other disciplines is so different from that applied to Radcliffe-Brown that an examination of the term is in order.

Like functionalism, structuralism, as Levi-Strauss uses it, is by no means confined to anthropology. Examples of scholars from other disciplines who are classified as structuralists are Freud, Marx, and Piaget. These people all have sought universal structures of human nature, though from different standpoints. Freud believed there were universal, psychological mechanisms and motives; Marx believed the universals were the production of necessities basic to life, economic universals; and Piaget researched in areas of child development which he believed showed universal patterns underlying cultural surface behavior. All structuralists have methodologies or techniques to decode and lay bare the structures. Freud used dreams and free association, for example. It has been suggested that structuralism may turn out to be a unifying approach to all the behavioral sciences.

As used by Levi-Strauss, structuralism means a search for deep, unapparent, innate structures of a psycho-biological nature universal to all human beings. These hidden infrastructures are very subtly manifest in surface behavior that varies greatly from culture to culture. The apparent behavior—culturally conditioned behavior—is observable but the deep structures are very difficult to uncover. To find them, one must first discover the proper rules of transformation and transpose the one set into the others. Many transformations may be required, for there are many layers or sets concealing the basic structure—the very structure of the human mind. Levi-Strauss does not claim to have found this yet.

Levi-Strauss believes that transformations are more readily performed in some areas than in others. He prefers art, language, and especially myth and he has drawn his methodological model from structural linguistics, analyzing forms of social activity as though they were languages. Underlying both language and social acts and relations are the structures of which the behaver is unconscious—grammer in the case of language. Thus, societies differ from one another just as their surface grammars differ but there is a deep, common structure, and that is what Levi-Strauss is seeking. (Noam Chomsky is pursuing this line of inquiry in linguistics.) Levi-Strauss believes basic thinking occurs as sets of contrasts: day, night; black, white; life, death; spirit, body, and so on. This dualism shows up in the super-structures in various ways—for instance, in moiety organization and in myths—and the deeper structures determine much that appears to be arbitrary or sheer chance.

Basic to the commonality of all humans, according to Levi-Strauss, is a mental demand for order, a universal impulse toward classification. While "primitive" classification may not coincide with our categories, it nevertheless imposes some sort of order on amorphous reality. Naming is one way of organizing (classifying) experience and perceptions and communicating them. Information is stored and transmitted through such systematization. People sharing in one such system of classification are participants in the same culture but those who do not share that particular culture still participate in a common foundation through the universal infrastructures posited by Levi-Strauss and that foundation makes possible communication across cultural boundaries.

Claude Levi-Strauss, 1908–
(Courtesy of French Cultural Services)

Levi-Strauss created quite a stir in anthropology. Some people virtually abandoned their own lines of enquiry and became his disciples. Others have responded most negatively to his ideas. The area of greatest criticism has come from those irrevocably dedicated to positivism, the scientific method of hypothesis testing and validation. Since few, if any, seem able to replicate Levi-Strauss' transforms, they question whether he has discovered universal structures so much as invented them. They question the value of such work if everyone comes up with different results. In fact, unless one is able to break away from the empirical mode, it is virtually impossible to do more than enjoy Levi-Strauss' erudition and imagination, for he appears to make unprovable assumptions about humans.

Another criticism against Levi-Strauss is that he has created a closed, mentally deterministic model but this is not substantially true. His preoccupation with deep structures does not preclude an explanation of surface or cultural variety as adaptation to other groups or to a wide range of environmental situations. In fact, no causal explanation of surface variation is necessarily excluded in his model. He is not attempting to explain diversity, though he recognizes its existence. He does not see deep structures as determinative and causal but rather as providing the basis for surface diversity.

It may seem at first glance that Levi-Strauss revived Bastian's *psychic unity of mankind* doctrine but careful comparison shows that is a wrong conclusion. *Psychic unity* postulated that all humans would respond much alike to the same stimulus, producing similar results the world over. Levi-Strauss says that though there are universal deep structures, human responses are widely dissimilar and the surface structures consequently show wide ranges of cultural behavior. Thus, it cannot be said with any accuracy that Levi-Strauss has created a closed system or taken a psycho-biological determinist stand. He has not. In fact, he has emphatically insisted that cultures are molded by their social and physical environments, though, like the basic biological endowment of *Homo sapiens*, he insists that there is also a universal mental endowment.

Levi-Strauss has also been innovative in kinship study. He was trained in the French tradition of Durkheim and from Durkheim's disciple, Mauss, Levi-Strauss took the idea of gift exchange and general reciprocity and applied it to kinship systems. His work on the structures of elementary kinship based on the exchange of women in marriage (women are the ultimate scarce good) created a whole new way of looking at marriage: alliance theory. Levi-Strauss proposed that elementary kinship systems are primarily means of regulating the exchange of women and creating alliances between groups. Dualism or binary discriminations show up in this reciprocal exchange through dichotomies of own-group and other-group, or wife-takers and wife-givers.

BRITISH ANTHROPOLOGY IN THE 60S

British social anthropology largely continued down paths indicated in the previous decade. Anthropologists showed greater interest in adding time depth to analysis and in the changing social structures as members of the former empire gained independence. (Independence for British overseas territories became routine in the 60s.) The one outstanding exception to the continuity with past orientations was Edmund Leach.

Leach found the structural-functional approach even less adequate than he had in the preceding decade. In an important article, "Rethinking Anthropology" (1961a), he declared that Radcliffe-Brown's type of comparative sociology was like butterfly collecting. He said Radcliffe-Brown typed social structures and then compared the types which Leach found arbitrary and artificial—like classification of butterflies by shape, size, color, or whatever categories the collector might impose. To Leach, such typology was meaningless for explanation because data were forced into analytic categories that might have no correspondence with reality—categories like patrilineal and matrilineal—to suit the classifier, not those so classified. Rather than generalize on such meaningless classes, Leach proposed an anthropology based on "inspired guesswork" which would hopefully lead to new insights and "unexpected conclusions." He suggested that generalization rather than comparison should be the goal of theory and proposed that beneath surface appearances, which are interpreted and consequently distorted according to the biases of the observers, there lie basic patterns which should be the object of research. He further posited that there may well be similarities in underlying patterns that are obscured by the surface distortions.

In Levi-Strauss' research and tentative conclusions, Leach found one possible direction anthropology might pursue to lift itself from structural-functional doldrums. He also believed that Levi-Strauss' work avoided ethnocentric biases. In recent years, Leach has considered himself Levi-Strauss' critic and interpreter to the English-speaking anthropological audience. Whatever reservation Levi-Strauss may have about his self-appointed foremost disciple, Leach has found something in the new structuralist approach that is creative and appealing and he has turned to this new line of enquiry with enthusiasm.

CULTURAL MATERIALISM

A notable theoretical shift in American anthropology in the 60s was a return to an interest in cultural causation—a search for regularities from which could be derived generalizations about human behavior. Prominent within this theoretical orientation were those seeking cultural causality in terms of environmental adaptation or the material bases of life. Both are cultural materialist strategies with techno-economic or techno-environmental factors as the independent variables. Looking at the technological means of maintaining life, cultural materialists applied their theories to history and behavior to show causal relations in culture change.

Return to Evolutionism

Though it was in the 60s that the movement—if it can be called that—toward generalization gathered momentum enough to be considered a major aspect of American anthropology, some reaction to Boas' particularism had emerged as early as the 30s.

Leslie White (1900–1975), a professor at the University of Michigan, had been trained in the Boasian cultural relativist and particularist tradition, but as a teacher, found it inadequate and confining. Students were seeking causal explanation and White believed they were entitled to answers. A series of events brought his attention to Tylor and Morgan, and after careful study of the nineteenth century evolutionist literature, he concluded that evolutionism was not wrong in theory, only in data and that cultural evolution was just as real and demonstrable as biological evolution. The change from simple to complex with greater specialization of the parts was just as real in cultural development as in physical but the problem was to find a universal standard of measurement—one that was not culture-bound. With some sort of scale, one could compare cultures and arrange them in a developmental sequence.

White suggested the control of energy by society as a standard, an idea not original with him but his application was new. He developed what he called the *Basic Law of Cultural Evolution*: culture evolves as the amount of energy harnessed per capita per year is increased, or as the efficiency of the instrumental means of putting energy to work is increased. He claimed he derived this from the second law of thermodynamics—the law of increasing entropy—which says in effect that in the universe as a whole, a tendency toward increasing randomness (more diffuse distribution of energy) exists, though in certain systems, entropy is reversed. That happens in biological systems and also in cultural systems and it means that increased concentration of energy results in greater complexity, specialization, and more parts.

Called "neo-evolutionism" by many, White's position as he saw it was nothing new but was merely based on better information and while he stimulated many students, White found little acceptance among his colleagues during his early years. Boasians like Lowie and Kroeber saw little merit in White's formulation and argued quite vigorously against his approach. White responded and relations between him and most of his peers were something less than cordial.

White suggested that anthropology is properly the science of culture; he called it *culturology*. He emphasized the importance of human usage of symbols and symbolization which he pointed out made possible the cultural mode of adaptation. And like Durkheim, he claimed that culture could be explained only in terms of culture, never by individual psychology. As a result, he is classified with Durkheim and Kroeber as a superorganicist. Psychology is an expression of culture, according to White, not its cause. Human nature is really cultural nature, and any explanation based on innate characteristics cannot be correct because such characteristics must be a constant, universal in all humans and a constant cannot explain a variable; *culture is a variable*. To the Boasians (like Sapir), who cried in anguish that White had eliminated people, White said that the question of who votes, who eats, and so on is an unproductive one. Of course it is individuals and not cultures. But the debatable question is: *why does one group eat something loathed by another group?* It is because of cultural conditioning.

To those who declared that his view was fatalistic or defeatist, White replied that he never claimed people were irrelevant; humans are prerequisite to culture. But each one is born into an ongoing cultural system and his choices are the options available within his culture. What he strives for is culturally determined but he will strive. White's attitude or philosophical position should not have antagonized the Boasians. They themselves have been classified as cultural determinists. If White had stated his position differently—if he had said merely that each human is the product of his enculturation processes—most Boasians would have found little to object to.

White perceived three cultural subsystems: *technological, sociological,* and *ideological.* The way society uses its technology to sustain life influences the sociological and ideological systems. Technology and therefore culture evolve as more energy is harnessed but though the original impulse comes from the technological system, all the systems, articulated and once in motion, are mutually involved in a positive feedback relationship.

Multilinear Evolution and Cultural Ecology

White was not alone in mid-twentieth century America in his search for regularities and causation. Julian Steward, who had been a student of both Lowie and Kroeber, also turned from a particularist orientation to greater generalization. Steward, however, found White's approach too broad to be useful for explanation because White's theory of energy capture could not explain why some cultures capture free energy while others do not.

It seemed to Steward that if identical operations were causing parallel cultural developments in widely separated areas, he ought to be able to discover not only the initial cause but causation in the successive stages by examining and comparing the sequences. Therefore, he proposed a search for limited regularities and suggested that anthropologists look for parallel changes in form and function occurring in similar environments to see whether any causal principles could be found. His approach was extremely empirical and his independent variables were environment and economy with social organization and ideology as the dependent variables. This was not too radical a departure from White's interacting subsystem model, in fact.

Steward tested out his formulation in areas so far separated that he could safely assume he had independent cases. He compared developments in the so-called cradles of civilization—the river areas of oldest agriculture in the Old World and areas of the New World where cultivation had led to urban developments. He found discernible regularities and developmental sequences broadly similar from earliest farming communities to conquest empires. He called his formulation *multilinear evolution* as compared to the unilineal evolutionism of the nineteenth century and he called the evolutionary schemes of White and V. G. Childe *universal evolution* because they were concerned with universal culture, not isolated cultures. Unlike the others, Steward proposed no universal stages.

Steward attributed the convergence he discovered in Old and New World civilization to cultural interaction with the environment. While he never claimed that environment was determinative, as clearly shown by the variety of human responses, he argued that human societies must react to environment; they cannot ignore it. In the course of adapting to environment, humans introduce a superorganic element: culture. Steward, seeing culture as a means of adaptation to environment, proposed the study of cultural ecology: the relationships among environment, the human organisms present, and the superorganic element—culture.

To control the many cultural variables in his approach, Steward suggested focusing on culture cores: those institutions and techniques most closely associated with environmental adaptation and exploitation. Cultures having similar core features belong to the same cultural type; that is, they show the same general responses to similar environments and are assumed to have the same structural and functional interrelationships. Levels of sociocultural complexity become apparent when cultural types are placed on a continuum of complexity. Steward suggested use of levels of sociocultural integration so that like units could be compared. He used the categories: family level, multifamily level, and state level, which were later refined to band, tribe, chiefdom, and state. Each level has different means of integration: kinship, associations, economic complementarity, and policing force and bureaucracy.

Steward also advanced the culture area formulation by classifying cultural types in terms of their ecological adaptations and historical developments. Unlike Kroeber and Wissler, he placed only secondary significance on culture traits and worked out a new culture area scheme for South America based on two sets of variables, adaptation and level of sociocultural complexity. His scheme proposed four areas: Marginal, Tropical Forest, Circum-Caribbean, and Andean. They were used as the organizational basis for his monumental production, *The Handbook of the South American Indians* (1946–1950), which he edited and also contributed articles.

Cultural ecology has found particular favor among archaeologists and some cultural anthropologists, for example, Andrew Vayda and Roy Rappaport, have further refined and elaborated Steward's work by analyzing the relationship between culture and environment as a form of feedback system.[1]

General and Specific Evolution

In the early 60s, Marshall Sahlins, Elman Service, and some other colleagues or followers of Steward and White tried to reconcile the two viewpoints. Drawing heavily on analogy with biological evolution, they suggested that evolution has two facets. One is general evolution, a grand movement from simple to complex; the other, specific evolution, change as an adaptive response to an ecological niche. Specific evolution leads to diversity through adaptation: in biology, to the various species; in society, to culture histories. Steward's multilinear evolution is specific.

---

[1] A feedback system is defined as one in which the result of a signal or series of signals is another one which modifies and directs the next. Negative feedback is self-damping, always such as to reduce error; positive feedback results in an intensification of the condition responsible for the primary action and leads to infinite build-up unless acted upon from the outside.

Cultural relativism is applicable to specific evolution, for each culture can be judged only relative to its ecological niche. General evolution, on the other hand, means abandoning relativism. General evolutionary change is absolute and can be judged by absolute criteria. White was talking about general evolution which can be evaluated or measured by the amount of energy harnessed.

Sahlins and Service went on to apply the biological analogy at greater length, though they carefully pointed out that in cultural evolution, change is additive, not substitutive, and can be transmitted by diffusion, a much faster means of dissemination than genetic transmission. As adaptation increases so does stability and the greater the specialization, the less potential for evolution. (Childe had made this point too.) A corollary is that evolutionary potential is greater in less adapted and less specialized societies. Specific evolution means increasing adaptation; general evolution means increasing adaptability.

Though both Steward and White used concepts of evolution, perhaps in light of the kind of explanation commonly sought today, the idea of evolution is less important than their turn to some type of techno-environmental causation where priority is given to the material basis of social life. Conflicts over the issues of evolutionism are really beside the point of the materialist approach which tries to see why things happen and what causes them, not to describe their developmental manifestations. The cultural materialist approach to theory became so widely used in the 60s in America (the British have resisted its appeal) that it now seems incredible that for so many years it was ignored or even derided. Perhaps the increasing concern for environment and interest in general ecology added to its attraction.

ETHOLOGY

Ethology is the science of animal behavior and is not a new interest or area of research since scientists of many disciplines have been studying animals in zoos, laboratories, or other artificial environments for a long time. However, in the late 50s and the 60s, many investigations were launched to study animals, especially nonhuman primates, ranging freely in their natural environments. Those field studies produced information about primate social organization unavailable from fossil remains or observation of animals in artificial situations. The studies, pursued in both the Old and New Worlds, have suggested how proto-humans may have behaved as well as offering reasons for that behavior. Anthropologists have become increasingly interested in ethological research and among the many excellent field studies on primates are those by Jane van Lawick-Goodall on chimpanzees, George Schaller on gorillas, and Irven DeVore on baboons.

For sociocultural anthropologists, ethological studies have pointed out the importance of environment in the development of various types of social organization and how ecological factors mediate social behavior. Ethologists have also gained insight into relationships among individual animals within the natural groups (for example, dominance hierarchies, and on the adaptive significance of social behavior and how the individual responds to group norms). These field studies have implications for a wide range of interests—for example, for students of population dynamics, for psychologists interested in the nature of thought processes, and for linguists studying nonverbal communication. In addition, ethology has caused a reappraisal of *Homo sapiens* as the tool-making animal since chimpanzees have been shown not only to use simple tools, but to make them.

CULTURAL RELATIVISM RECONSIDERED

As anthropology developed in England and America in the twentieth century, students were trained in the belief that the proper research stance was one of detachment when questions of value, change, ranking, and the like arose. The fieldworker and classroom lecturer should neither support nor oppose change— or in fact, make any value judgments about any culture other than his own. This, of course, was an ethical position growing out of a belief in cultural relativism, at one time considered an indispensable component of anthropology. However, in the 60s and even before, the ideology of cultural relativism and noninvolvement came under attack. It was not that anthropologists began to think that some cultures were intrinsically more worthy than others but rather that they became aware of certain contradictions inherent in the relativist position. Some thought humane value judgments should be made: Is not a society without poverty (or slavery, disease, and so on) better than one with it? The relativist position, rigidly adhered to, precluded an answer.

Logical inconsistencies in the relativist argument could not be ignored. If facts were relative to their cultural matrix, how could an anthropologist claim anthropology was an objective science? Anthropologists claimed that tolerance was good, but what of the society that is intolerant? Should they tolerate intolerance? Bigotry? Relativists appeared to consider relativism an absolute good while denying the existence of any absolute. If there are no common values, can mutual respect endure? Conflicts of this nature led to the proposal that relativism must be maintained as a methodological tool, necessary to understand other cultures free of personal bias, but that it should not be considered prescriptive as an ideology.

Going beyond the separation of relativism as methodology and as ideology, belief developed on the part of a growing number of anthropologists that they should be more involved with changing conditions in the world—more committed to eliminating inequalities in human life. Some took the stand that wherever the underdeveloped nations or deprived peoples wished help with industrialization or development programs, anthropologists should be in the vanguard directing change. To act otherwise would be to abdicate responsibility. To try to preserve societies as fossil cultures would be absurd as well as impossible. And if change were inevitable, was it not preferable that anthropologists should do their share to make it as painless as possible?

Some professionals have gone far beyond just offering help; they urge active intervention to generate change and they advocate abandoning any pretense to "value-free" inquiry. They believe anthropology has lost its relevance, that it must be "reinvented," and that it must become partisan politically and ethnically (Hymes 1972: *passim*). Others have thought such a change would destroy anthropology as a science and they ask, "Whose politics, whose ethics?" (Kaplan 1974). This debate will most certainly continue for some time, perhaps decades.

7

The Past and the Future

Topics of research pertinent to sociocultural anthropology today have origins in earlier ideas and beliefs, some several centuries old. Those ideas have been modified and expanded as the result of new knowledge and contacts among peoples of diverse backgrounds. While no one will deny new forms and new challenges, neither will any thoughtful person deny that the past persists in the present. To trace contemporary threads back to their original fabric is often fascinating; to see the changes and new directions is likewise intriguing.

Although it is an arbitrary beginning, we start with the Age of Exploration—the sixteenth through the eighteenth centuries—when European nations sent explorers, merchants, missionaries and military personnel to all corners of the earth. Those people met other humans whose existence was unknown in Europe and whose lifeways were often vastly different. Reports, often exaggerated and frequently erroneous, excited European curiosity about other cultures and traditional anthropological interest in non-Western peoples may be traced to this period of exploration.

Europeans, not unnaturally, sought explanations for the great variety in human ways that had been reported. What makes people different is a question with a long history, a question that is basic to sociocultural anthropology. A companion question has been, of course, what is the extent of human likeness; for example, what do all humans hold in common? Interest in common human structures as well as in human diversity was greatly stimulated by the three centuries of exploration.

In the eighteenth century, in addition to a more casual, popular curiosity in other cultures, many of the greatest minds in Europe began to ponder about the nature of the world and of human beings. During this period, the Enlightenment philosophers debated whether people were born good, bad, or neutral; but debate was minimal over the question of progress—that seemed apparent—and it generated many schemes explaining the development of the history of man.

In the physical sciences, the scientific method resulted in experimentation under controlled conditions and the social philosophers tried to apply the scientific method to the study of man. As the physical scientists strove to know natural laws, so the social philosophers sought universal laws governing human nature. Even so, the study of both the diversity and the universality of human ways was hardly objective. It was virtually self-evident that European life was superior, though the eighteenth century was marked with general belief that others' inferiority was not innate and could therefore be overcome as they learned to be more like Europeans. However, the attempt to apply the scientific notion of objectivity to the study of society did help to counteract the assumption of European superiority.

In the nineteenth century, social philosophy and scientific advances from the Enlightenment led to social physics and then to sociology—Auguste Comte's terms for the application of scientific method to the study of man. The notion of progress, also coming from the Enlightenment, stimulated Comte and a number of others to describe human history in a series of evolutionary stages of increasing complexity and heterogeneity. The idea of social evolution or progress was commonplace before Darwin published his theory of biological evolution which was not well received by the general public, but which Herbert Spencer and some others hailed as substantiating the social evolutionary position. The Romantic Movement and the concomitant swing from the skepticism of the Enlightenment to a more fundamentalist approach to religion meant much popular opposition to the idea of bioevolution and a preference for catastrophism as an explanation of change in forms. Though the scientific community favored acceptance of bioevolution, that theory contributed little to social evolutionism before the twentieth century.

What is human nature? What is learned, what is innate? These questions ran like a lode of ore in a mine through social thought following the Enlightenment. Sociologists tried to find answers by investigating their own society. Anthropologists, on the other hand, sought a broader range: humanity around the world. But in the infancy of the discipline, the search was often submerged in the question of origins: how did institutions and customs arise? Today considered by many an intellectual dead end, this search for beginnings commanded anthropological attention for fully half a century.

The last half of the nineteenth century saw the development of professional anthropology and theory that was specifically anthropological. L. H. Morgan in the United States and E. B. Tylor in England were the prime figures, both operating within a social evolutionary framework. They were interested in the totality of culture—not in specific cultural systems—and Tylor's emphasis on culture and learned behavior became the hallmark of American anthropology in the following century.

The general nineteenth century evolutionist position was that human culture had evolved through successively progressive or increasingly complex stages. The content of the sequences was much the same for all; non-Western peoples were used as examples of the earlier stages; and the notion of psychic unity indicated that the basic psychological structures for advancement were common to all people.

Growing reaction to the abuses of nineteenth century classical evolutionist positions resulted in the early twentieth century in objections to the rigidity of the psychic unity doctrine, to the idea of stages of set content for all people, and above all to the lack of factual foundations for the sweeping generalizations typical of the unilineal evolutionists. Everywhere anthropologists began to urge the necessity of gathering one's own data through intensive fieldwork.

In America, anthropology under Franz Boas turned toward meticulous data collection in the field and careful historical investigation of specific societies to determine the presumably unique series of events that led to each manifestation— historical particularism. Culture was the unifying concept of American anthropology as it developed under Boas and the goal was total coverage—all aspects of culture in addition to culture history. Each society, Boas warned, could be judged only in its own terms; values were relative to their cultural matrix. Boas at first cautioned against premature generalization but eventually he became skeptical that generalization about human behavior would ever be possible.

Boas' students followed his position that each individual was what his culture made him and they emphasized Boas' stand on cultural relativism; that each culture could be understood only in its own terms and could therefore not be compared to any other. The hallmarks of the Boasian position were its emphasis on human plasticity and cultural uniqueness and diversity. The position was a needed corrective to racism and ethnocentrism, yet it also led to rigidity and ultimately to theoretical sterility. Most of Boas' students who are remembered today broke away from the extreme atomistic stance of historical particularism.

In Austro-Germany, a diffusionist school looked for culture complexes or culture circles and their spread through time and space and in France, sociology under Emile Durkheim was characterized by interest in the integration of society through beliefs and symbols shared by its members. Using cross-cultural data in his work, Durkheim took a functional approach to social interactions, seeing institutions as they operated within the whole.

In England the British were greatly influenced by Durkheim. Anthropologists saw little merit in any historical approach and A. R. Radcliffe-Brown's focus was synchronic examination of how parts of the social structure functioned to maintain the whole and on cross-cultural comparisons among societies, while Bronislaw Malinowski sought to analyze the way institutions functioned to supply the needs of individuals. Though Malinowski called himself a functionalist and Radcliffe-Brown is usually referred to as a structural-functionalist, they shared the view that any attempt to study parts of the organic whole (culture in the case of Malinowski, structure in the case of Radcliffe-Brown) in isolation would result in distortion. The two men reacted not only to classical evolutionism but also to the American particularism which seemed to them in danger of fragmenting cultures in order to trace unique historical development by tracing diffusion of traits through time and space. Traits cannot be abstracted from context but must be studied as they interact. They sought instead to demonstrate coherence and integration within societies.

Britons, like Americans, urged long and careful fieldwork to gather the data so woefully lacking in the preceding century. Malinowski contributed the methodology of participant-observation to the discipline. He brought fieldwork to a new degree of excellence but it was Radcliffe-Brown who had the greater impact on the development of theory in Britain and America.

Though Radcliffe-Brown and Malinowski both chose a synchronic approach, there was nothing in functionalism intrinsically incompatible with a study of change and by midcentury, some British anthropologists turned to a more dia-chronic approach. A few, like Forde and Firth, expanded into environmental and economic studies, though in general, synchronic functional analysis remained the hallmark of British social anthropology. In America, however, the midcentury was marked by burgeoning expansion geographically and research into studies like accul-turation, coded data retrieval, and an interest in culture and personality and the ap-plication of psychological theories and techniques cross culturally. In general, the American focus was on cultural diversity and the Americans continued to show a predilection for the concept of culture though the British, for the most part, found that concept unwieldy and vague, selecting *society* as more to their taste. With the exception of Malinowski, the holistic American approach to the dis-cipline had little appeal across the Atlantic.

In the period following the Second World War, American culture and per-sonality studies changed from attempts to see how society socialized the young into approved adult personality types to a new interest in cognitive processes. An important facet of cognitive studies was the ethnoscience movement which brought to a head a controversy that had been simmering for some decades: *What is the nature of culture; is it real or a mental construct?* The problem of real versus ideal was an old one. The Enlightenment philosophers and even the ancient Greek thinkers had recognized the problem with which ethnoscientists and other anthro-pologists grappled: what is real—the thing or the perception of it? The gap be-tween perception and scientific description has caused concern for centuries. Some anthropologists think that knowledge can come only from each individual's per-ception of reality; others claim that behavior is all we can observe and our con-clusions must be based solely on behavioral data. Though these two positions have not been reconciled, two terms—*emic* and *etic*—have come into use to indicate the folk perception and the analytic view respectively and many ethnologists have concluded that the best reporting of anthropological data would include both.

The Boasian emphasis on human plasticity and diversity began to give way in America after World War II as a new interest in human universals arose. Some old questions were restated and the answers were sought within the human psyche as well as in studies of culture as adaptation. Do human responses after all have set limits? What is the nature of mankind? Both the cultural materialist and various cognitive approaches were applied to those questions and by the 60s, most Ameri-can anthropologists had moved away from the anti-theoretical orientation of the early century to a search for regularities and greater generalization. British an-thropology remained far less eclectic and experimental, though some British anthro-pologists became interested in the structuralism of Levi-Strauss.

Claude Levi-Strauss became very influential in both America and Britain in the 60s when his works became available in English translation. Proposing a search for the fundamental structures of the human mind, Levi-Strauss suggested the use of structural linguistics as a model for transformation techniques that would strip away the diverse surface (cultural) layers eventually to reveal the universal struc-tures of human nature. Though popular today with many, Levi-Strauss has his detractors, too; many trained in the empirical tradition find it difficult to accept work that cannot be verified.

Today most anthropologists would probably agree that no one theoretical stance holds all the answers. British, American, and French anthropologists have enriched one another's thinking and there is no hard-line division or consistent difference among them. It is likewise the case that theoretical orientations are not mutually exclusive. Cultural ecology, for example, does not necessarily rule out cognitive studies or functionalism. And while most American and British anthropologists have been trained within the scientific or empirical tradition, many have been willing to abandon positivism at least long enough to enjoy the creative dialectics of Levi-Strauss. Furthermore, many professionals find nothing distasteful in taking into account both materialist and idealist points of view. Perhaps the profession has reached a maturity that dictates renouncing the search for one path to ultimate truth.

THE FUTURE

What role will anthropology play as academic goals and structures change? I think it will have an increasingly important impact on education. Already anthropology has entered the curricula of many high schools and a few primary and junior high schools, though on the last two levels, older titles like social science have usually been retained. On the college level, where philosophy and the classics no longer act as synthesizers of thought, many see the gap left by the traditional disciplines filled by anthropology which has achieved a grand sweep and holistic approach to human behavior.

Traditionally, anthropologists have been researchers and have rarely tried to effect or direct change themselves. Quite the contrary, they usually have made every effort to avoid causing any disturbance in the societies they study and many consider preservation of the traditional ways or the *status quo ante* the proper goal. However, since World War II, anthropologists have been much more actively involved with problem solving in cities and among the underdeveloped nations, as the increasing frequency of the terms *applied anthropology, urban anthropology,* and *action anthropology* implies. This trend will doubtless strengthen. In addition, the traditional subjects of anthropology—the "untouched primitives," the "non-literates," and small scale tribal people—are now largely a part of a cosmopolitan world culture with many of the same problems faced by people of industrial societies. It seems certain that anthropology must turn increasingly to studies of complex societies and their problems.

Until after World War II, most frequently anthropologists were Europeans investigating non-Western societies; today many non-Europeans are entering the profession. We can confidently expect that new, fresh ideas will enter with them, though we cannot say just what changes they will effect.

What all this means for new directions in theory is unclear because it is difficult to discern major theoretical change while it is gathering momentum. At the turn of the century, F. W. Maitland, an historian, suggested that anthropology must become history or it would become nothing. Recently, in light of the disappearing non-industrial peoples, it has been said that anthropology will become sociology. There are reasons that the latter prediction probably will not come true any more than the first did. The breadth and holistic nature of anthropology will maintain its distinctiveness from sociology which tends to focus on more restricted topics and does not include the time depth and biological aspects of human behavior. In addition, most anthropologists would deny that the objects of their studies are only primitives, or colonial peoples, or exotic societies. They would rightly insist that anthropology is mankind studying itself and its problems and it certainly does not appear that we will run out of problems in the very near future.

What then is one theoretical direction we might reasonably expect? Levi-Strauss has revitalized the age-old interest in basic human nature and I do not think that this interest has yet run its course. Indeed, this form of structuralism seems to be attracting ethnologists who previously had shown quite different theoretical learnings: Edmund Leach and Marshall Sahlins, for example. Interest from people so distinguished cannot be easily dismissed. Perhaps some blending of cultural materialism with the search for universal infrastructures—a combination of techno-environmental and biopsychological variables—will mark the next theoretical move in the profession; perhaps this will involve more testing of Freudian theories cross culturally. Such a combination of materialism and structuralism could herald the formulation of a field theory that will encompass all behavioral science.

Glossary

Acculturation: The process of culture change as a result of long term, face-to-face contact between two societies.

Age-area hypothesis: The hypothesis that older elements have a wider distribution and the probable site of origin is that with the greatest concentration of traits.

Animism: A belief in spirits; Tylor's minimal definition of religion.

Anomie: Normlessness; cultural alienation (Durkheim).

Apollonian: Serene, peaceful, moderate; used by Ruth Benedict to describe the Zuni Indians.

Approach: The relative emphasis in theory and method or the criteria used by a scholar in research; orientation.

Assimilation: Absorption of a group into the ways of the dominant society and the group's general loss of cultural distinctiveness as a result.

Cognition: The processes of thinking and perceiving; knowledge.

Collective conscience: The beliefs and sentiments shared by members of a society (Durkheim).

Comparative method (applied to classical evolutionism):   The practice of equating living tribal groups with archaic or primordial society.

Configurationism: The theory that each society has a cluster or constellation of characteristics that identify it and set it apart from others.

Convergence: The production of similar final states from originally different starting points or conditions.

Correlation: Mutual relations among phenomena; systematic connections.

Cross cultural: Pertaining to diverse cultures; systematic comparison among several societies.

Cultural ecology: Relationships among humans, their culture, and the environment.

Cultural evolution: The transformation of cultural forms into more complex forms.

Cultural materialism: The theory of cultural causation in which technology, economics, and environment are considered the independent variables.

Cultural relativism: The position that there is no universal standard to measure cultures, that all cultures are equally valid and must be understood in their own terms.

Culture area: A geographic region in which cultures are significantly similar.

Culture center: The point of greatest concentration of the most typical traits of the culture area.

Culture circle: English translation of *Kulturkreis*; the area or location of a complex of culture traits in the usage of the Austro-German diffusionists.

Culture core: The institutions and techniques most closely associated with environmental adaptation and exploitation (Steward).

Culture type: A classification by cultural core features (Steward).

Culturology: The scientific study of culture (Leslie White).

Deductive: Reasoning from generalizations to specific or more concrete conclusions.

101

Degeneration: The theory of the "fall of man" from some original divine or innocent state; also called degradation.

Determinism (in social science):   Explanation by means of a single, simplistic causation.

Diachronic: Pertaining to events or phenomena as they change or exist over time.

Dialectics: Georg Hegel's philosophy of change through the resolution of opposites: the central tendency or thesis opposed by its opposite, antithesis, resolved in a synthesis which becomes a new thesis generating an antithesis, and so on.

Diffusion: Transmission of cultural traits from one person or group to another; cultural borrowing.

Divergence: The production of varied final conditions from originally similar states.

Dysfunction: A maladaptive or stressful function.

Emic: Pertaining to the view from within the culture, the folk view; meanings in terms of native categories.

Enculturation: The processes of becoming competent in one's culture. In contrast to socialization, which usually applies to the childhood years, enculturation is thought of as continuing throughout one's life.

Endogamy: The rule or law of marriage with someone within one's own group.

Enlightenment: The period from the last part of the seventeenth century through the eighteenth century; a time of important philosophical and scientific development.

Ethnocentrism: The practice of using one's own cultural values as the standard to measure all other cultures and a belief in the inherent superiority of one's own culture.

Ethnography: The description or documentation of a culture.

Ethnohistory: The reconstruction of the history of societies (usually nonliterate) based upon information gleaned from oral traditions, written materials from outsiders, linguistic and archaeological data, or any other form of pertinent information.

Ethnology: The theoretical analysis of culture in comparative perspective.

Ethnoscience: An attempt at cultural description from a totally emic standpoint, eliminating all the ethnographer's own categories.

Ethology: The study of animal behavior in natural habitats.

Etic: Pertaining to the view of an outside, scientific observer; the analytic view, presumably replicable by any trained observer.

Eufunction: A positive, adaptive function.

Exogamy: The rule or law of marriage with someone outside one's own group.

Experimental method: See scientific method.

Feedback system: A system in which the result of a signal or series of signals is another signal which modifies and directs the next.

Functionalism: The approach that explains social phenomena in terms of their integrative relationships and contributions to the maintenance of society or to the needs of individuals rather than in terms of causation.

Gemeinschaft: Community (Tönnies).

Genealogical method: Techniques for obtaining information about sociological patterns while eliciting the kinship terms and relationships of a society (Rivers).

Generalization: A statement that something is true or typical of a class of things.

Gesellschaft: Society (Tönnies).

Humanism: A philosophy or ethical system centered on the concepts of the dignity, freedom, and value of human beings.

Hypothesis: A statement of plausible connections among specific elements.

Idealism: The theoretical position that phenomena and events exist only in so far as they are perceived as ideas.

Idiographic: Particularistic, unique; specific as opposed to generalizing.

Inductive: Pertaining to reasoning from a number of specific cases to a law or generalization.

Kulturkreislehre: The Austro-German diffusionist theory of culture circles.

Matriarchy: Rule by women.

Matrilineality (Matriliny):   The reckoning of descent through women only.

Mesolithic (Middle Stone Age):   The period from the end of the Ice Age (the Pleistocene) to the introduction of domestication (usually applied only to Europe).

Model: A generalized picture, analogy, or explanation of reality.

Monogenesis: The theory that all humans are one species with a common ancestor.

Multilinear evolutionism: The term applied to Julian Steward's theory of cultural evolution.

Natural law: Law according to nature, independent of the laws of man.

Natural selection: The principle that the organisms which are best adapted to their environments will live to reproduce the most viable offspring. The primary mechanism of evolutionary change.

Neoevolutionism: The term sometimes applied to Leslie White's theories of cultural evolution.

Neolithic (New Stone Age):   Period characterized by the introduction of domesticated plants and animals.

New Ethnography: An alternate term for "ethnoscience."

Nomothetic: Producing generalizations or laws.

Oedipus complex: The Freudian theory of conflict and ambivalence between father and son with rivalry for the affection of the mother and wife.

Organic analogy: The comparison of society with an organism.

Orientation: See approach.

Paleolithic (Old Stone Age):   A period of stone technology confined to chipping and flaking.

Parallel evolution: The evolution of the same trait or characteristic independently in more than one culture or place.

Participant-observation: The anthropological method of fieldwork involving observation of a society while participating in the lifeways of the people as much as possible.

Patriarchy: Rule by men.

Patrilineality (Patriliny):   The reckoning of descent through males only.

Polygenesis: The theory that humans belong to several species, descended from different ancestors.

Positivism: The philosophy developed by Auguste Comte stating that reality can be apprehended objectively and that explanation in the social sciences can and should be as objective and empirical as in the natural sciences. Positivism excludes all metaphysical speculation.

Projective test: A test which calls forth a projection of the subject's own inner state and feelings as he responds to an ambiguous stimulus.

Psychic unity of mankind: English translation of Bastian's term *Elementargedanken*; the concept that all humans have the same basic potential to respond in the same way to similar stimuli, moderated only by local conditions.

Racism: The belief that races possess genetically inherited characteristics that determine their culture.

Reductionism: Explanation of phenomena in terms of a simpler level of organization.

Revitalization: A conscious effort by members of society to create more satisfying lifeways.

Rorschach test: A projective test in which the subject interprets a standardized set of ink-blots.

Scientific method: Methodology based on observation, classification, controlled experimentation, and hypothesizing.

Social Darwinism: Application of the concepts of biological evolution and the struggle for survival to social behavior and society.

Socialization: The patterns of child-rearing in the behaviors approved by society.

Structural-functionalism: The theoretical position that social parts are integrated and function to maintain the structural whole (Radcliffe-Brown).

Structuralism (French):   A philosophy holding that there are nonapparent, innate psycho-biological structures common to all human beings (Levi-Strauss).

Superorganic: The realm of culture or behavior considered as a thing in and of itself, independent of human beings.

Survivals: Traces in later times of older practices, beliefs, or items that have lost their functions (Tylor).

Synchronic: Having a single time plane, limited in time; nonhistorical.

Syncretism: The fusion of two or more systems of belief and ritual.

Thematic Apperception Test (TAT):   A projective test composed of ambiguous pictures about which the subject makes up a story.

Theory: A statement that accounts for causes or relationships among phenomena.

Totemism: The belief in a sacred ancestor—perhaps a plant or animal—with whom the descendants are in a special, mystical relationship.

Variable: (1) Dependent: any element whose behavior is controlled by another; (2) Independent: any element that produces change or reaction in another.

Bibliography

I. HISTORIES

Bidney, David, 1967, *Theoretical Anthropology*. (2d ed.) New York: Schocken.

Brew, J. O., ed., 1968, *One Hundred Years of Anthropology*. Cambridge: Harvard University Press.

Daniel, Glyn, 1964, *The Idea of Prehistory*. Baltimore: Penguin.

Fortes, Meyer, 1953, *Social Anthropology at Cambridge since 1900*. Cambridge, England: Cambridge University Press.

Greene, John C., 1961, *The Death of Adam*. New York: Mentor.

Haddon, Alfred C., 1934, *History of Anthropology*. London: Watts.

Harris, Marvin, 1968, *The Rise of Anthropological Theory*. New York: Crowell.

Hatch, Elvin, 1973, *Theories of Man and Culture*. New York: Columbia University Press.

Kaplan, David, and Robert A. Manners, 1972, *Culture Theory*. Englewood Cliffs, N.J.: Prentice-Hall.

Kardiner, Abram, and Edward Preble, 1961, *They Studied Man*. New York: Mentor.

Kroeber, Alfred, and Clyde Kluckhohn, 1963, Culture: *A Critical Review of Concepts and Definitions*. New York: Vintage Books.

Langness, Lewis L., 1974, *The Study of Culture*. San Francisco: Chandler and Sharp.

Lowie, Robert H., 1937, *The History of Ethnological Theory*. New York: Rinehart.

Malefijt, Annemarie de Waal, 1974, *Images of Man*. New York: Knopf.

Murphy, Robert F., 1971, *The Dialectics of Social Life*. New York: Basic Books.

Stocking, George W., Jr., 1968, *Race, Culture and Evolution*. New York: The Free Press.

Voget, Fred W., 1975, *A History of Ethnology*. New York: Holt, Rinehart and Winston.

II. BOOKS OF READINGS

Bohannan, Paul J., and Mark Glazer, eds., 1973, *High Points in Anthropology*. New York: Knopf.

Darnell, Regna, ed., 1974, *Readings in the History of Anthropology*. New York: Harper & Row.

Firth, Raymond, ed., 1960, *Man and Culture: An Evaluation of the Work of Bronislaw Malinowski*. London: Routledge and Kegan Paul.

Fried, Morton H., ed., 1968, *Readings in Anthropology*. (2d ed.) 2 vols. New York: Crowell.

Gamst, Frederick, and Edward Norbeck, eds., 1976, *Ideas of Culture*. New York: Holt, Rinehart and Winston.

Hodgen, Margaret T., ed., 1964, *Early Anthropology in the Sixteenth and Seventeenth Centuries*. Philadelphia: University of Pennsylvania Press.

Hymes, Dell, ed., 1972, *Reinventing Anthropology*. New York: Pantheon.

Manners, Robert A., and David Kaplan, eds., 1968, *Theory in Anthropology: A Sourcebook*. Chicago: Aldine.

Moore, Frank W., ed., 1961, *Readings in Cross-cultural Methodology*. New Haven: Human Relations Area File Press.

Romney, A. Kimball, and Roy D'Andrade, eds., 1964, "Transcultural studies in cognition." *American Anthropologist*, 66, number 3, part 2.

Slotkin, James S., ed., 1965, "Readings in early anthropology." *Viking Fund Publications in Anthropology, number 40*. New York: Wenner-Gren Foundation.

III. AUTHORS CITED

Bachofen, Johann J., 1861, *Das Mutterrecht*. Basel, Switzerland: Benno Schwabe.

Bastian, Adolf, 1860, *Der Mensch in der Geschicte*. Leipzig, Germany: O. Wigand.

———, 1895, *Ethnische Elementargedanken in der Lehre vom Menschen*. Berlin: Weidmann'sche Buchhandlung.

Benedict, Ruth, 1932, "Configurations of culture in North America." *American Anthropologist*, 34:1–27.

———, 1934a, *Patterns of Culture*. Boston: Houghton Mifflin.

———, 1934b, "Anthropology and the abnormal." *Journal of General Psychology*, 10:59–79.

———, 1946, *The Chrysanthemum and the Sword*. Boston: Houghton Mifflin.

Bidney, David, 1944, "The concept of culture and some cultural fallacies." *American Anthropologist*, 46:30–44.

———, 1946, "The concept of cultural crisis." *American Anthropologist*, 48:534–51.

Boas, Franz, 1927, *Primitive Art*. Oslo: H. Ashehoug and Company.

———, 1938, *The Mind of Primitive Man* (rev. ed.). New York: Macmillan.

———, 1940, *Race Language and Culture*. New York: Macmillan.

———, 1964, *The Central Eskimo*. Lincoln, Nebraska: University of Nebraska Press.

Childe, Vere Gordon, 1925, *The Dawn of Western Civilization*. New York: Knopf.

———, 1946, *What Happened in History*. New York: Pelican Books.

———, 1951, *Man Makes Himself*. New York: Mentor.

———, 1963, *Social Evolution*. Cleveland: Meridian.

Dalton, George, 1969, "Theoretical issues in economic anthropology." *Current Anthropology*, 10:63–102.

Darwin, Charles, 1859, *The Origin of Species*. London: John Murray.

———, 1871, *The Descent of Man and Selection in Relation to Sex*. New York: D. Appleton.

Darwin, Charles, and Alfred R. Wallace, 1859, "On the tendency of species to form varieties; and on the perpetuation of varieties and species by natural means of selection." *Journal of the Linnaean Society*, 3:45–63.

Deloria, Vine, 1969, *Custer Died for Your Sins*. New York: Macmillan.

DeVore, Irven, ed., 1965, *Primate Behavior*. New York: Holt, Rinehart and Winston.

Douglas, Mary, 1973, *Natural Symbols*. New York: Vintage Books.

DuBois, Cora, 1944, *The People of Alor*. Minneapolis: University of Minnesota Press.

Durkheim, Emile, 1958, *The Rules of the Sociological Method*. Glencoe: The Free Press.

———, 1960, *The Division of Labor in Society*. Glencoe: The Free Press.

———, 1963, *Suicide*. Glencoe: The Free Press.

————, 1965, *The Elementary Forms of the Religious Life*. New York: The Free Press.

Durkheim, Emile, and Marcel Mauss, 1963, *Primitive Classification*. Chicago: University of Chicago Press.

Eggan, Fred, 1950, *Social Organization of the Western Pueblos*. Chicago: University of Chicago Press.

————, 1954, "Social anthropology and the method of controlled comparison." *American Anthropologist*, 56:743–63.

Engels, Friedrich, 1942, *The Origin of the Family, Private Property and the State*. New York: International Publishers.

Evans-Pritchard, Edward E., 1956, *Nuer Religion*. Oxford: Clarendon Press.

————, 1964, *Social Anthropology*. Glencoe: The Free Press.

Firth, Raymond, 1929, *Primitive Economics of the New Zealand Maori*. London: George Routledge.

————, 1963, *We, the Tikopia*. Boston: Beacon Press.

————, 1964, *Essays on Social Organization and Values*. London: Athalone Press.

Forde, C. Daryll, 1963, *Habitat, Economy and Society*. New York: Dutton.

Fortes, Meyer, 1969, *Kinship and the Social Order: The Legacy of Lewis Henry Morgan*. Chicago: Aldine.

Frazer, James, 1910, *Totemism and Exogamy*. London: Macmillan.

————, 1959, *The New Golden Bough* (abridged ed.). New York: Criterion.

Freud, Sigmund, 1928, *The Future of an Illusion*. London: Institute of Psychoanalysis.

————, 1930, *Civilization and its Discontents*. New York: Jonathan Cape and Harrison Smith.

————, 1938, *Totem and Taboo*. London: Penguin Books.

Frobenius, Leo, 1898, *Die Weltanschauung der Naturvölker*. Weimar, Germany: E. Felber.

Geertz, Clifford, 1966, "Religion as a cultural system." In Michael Banton, ed., *Anthropological Approaches to the Study of Religion*. London: Tavistock.

————, 1973, *The Interpretation of Cultures*. New York: Basic Books.

Gluckman, Max, 1955, *Custom and Conflict in Africa*. Oxford: Basil Blackwell.

————, 1962, *Essays on the Ritual of Social Relations*. Manchester: Manchester University Press.

————, 1963, *Order and Rebellion in Tribal Africa*. New York: The Free Press.

Goodenough, Ward, 1956, "Componential analysis and the study of meaning." *Language*, 32:195–216.

Graebner, Fritz, 1911, *Methode der Ethnologie*. Heidelberg: Carl Winter's Universitäts Buchhandlung.

Hallowell, A. I., 1955, *Culture and Experience*. Philadelphia: University of Pennsylvania Press.

Haviland, William A., 1975, *Cultural Anthropology*. New York: Holt, Rinehart and Winston.

Herskovits, Melville J., 1948, *Man and His Works*. New York: Knopf.

————, 1952, *Economic Anthropology*. New York: Knopf.

————, 1953, *Franz Boas: The Science of Man in the Making*. New York: Charles Scribner's Sons.

Hsu, Francis L. K., ed., 1972, *Psychological Anthropology*. (Rev. ed.), Cambridge, Mass.: Schenkman.

Kaplan, David, 1974, "The anthropology of authenticity." *American Anthropologist*, 76:824–839.

Kardiner, Abram, 1939, *The Individual and His Society*. New York: Columbia University Press.

Kardiner, Abram, *et al.*, 1945, *The Psychological Frontiers of Society.* New York: Columbia University Press.

Kluckhohn, Clyde, 1939, "The place of theory in anthropological studies." *The Philosophy of Science*, 6:328–44.

———, 1941, "Patterning as exemplified in Navaho culture." In Leslie Spier, ed., *Language, Culture, and Personality.* Wisconsin: Sapir Memorial Fund.

———, 1949, *Mirror for Man.* New York: McGraw-Hill.

———, 1952, "Values and value-orientations." In Talcott Parsons and Edward A. Shils, eds., *The Theory of Action.* Cambridge: Harvard University Press.

Kluckhohn, Florence R., and Fred L. Strodtbeck, 1961, *Variations in Value Orientations.* Evanston: Row, Peterson and Company.

Kroeber, Alfred L., 1917, "The superorganic." *American Anthropologist*, 19:163–213.

———, 1919, "On the principle of order in civilization as exemplified by changes of fashion." *American Anthropologist*, 21:235–63.

———, 1939, *Cultural and Natural Areas of Native North America.* Berkeley: University of California Press.

———, 1944, *Configurations of Culture Growth.* Berkeley and Los Angeles: University of California Press.

———, 1948, "White's view of culture." *American Anthropologist*, 50:405–415.

———, 1952, *The Nature of Culture.* Chicago: University of Chicago Press.

———, 1957, *Style and Civilizations.* Ithaca: Cornell University Press.

Lafitau, J. T., 1724, *Moeurs des Sauvages Amériquains Comparées aux Moeurs des Premiers Temps.* Paris: Saugrain l'aîné.

Leach, Edmund, 1954, *Political Systems of Highland Burma.* Cambridge: Harvard University Press.

———, 1961a, *Rethinking Anthropology.* London: Athalone Press.

———, 1961b, "Levi-Strauss in the Garden of Eden." *Transactions of the New York Academy of Sciences*, 23:386–96.

———, 1966, "On the founding fathers." *Current Anthropology*, 7:560–76.

Levi-Strauss, Claude, 1963, *Structural Anthropology.* New York: Basic Books.

———, 1966, *The Savage Mind.* Chicago: University of Chicago Press.

———, 1969, *The Elementary Structures of Kinship.* Boston: Beacon Press.

Levy-Bruhl, Lucien, 1966, *Primitive Mentality.* Boston: Beacon Press.

Lewis, Oscar, 1951, *Life in a Mexican Village.* Urbana: University of Illinois Press.

Lowie, Robert H., 1917, *Culture and Ethnology.* New York: McMurtrie.

———, 1920, *Primitive Society.* New York: Liveright Publishing Corp.

———, 1927, *The Origin of the State.* New York: Harcourt.

———, 1948, *Social Organization.* New York: Rinehart.

Maine, Henry Sumner, 1963, *Ancient Law.* Boston: Beacon Press.

Malinowski, Bronislaw, 1939, "The group and individual in functional analysis." *American Journal of Sociology*, 44:938–64.

———, 1954, *Magic, Science, and Religion, and other Essays.* Garden City, N.Y.: Doubleday.

———, 1955, *Sex and Repression in Savage Society.* New York: The Noonday Press.

———, 1960, *A Scientific Theory of Culture and other Essays.* New York: Oxford University Press.

———, 1961, *Argonauts of the Western Pacific.* New York: Dutton.

———, 1967, *A Diary in the Strict Sense of the Term.* New York: Harcourt.

Marx, Karl, 1888, *The Communist Manifesto.* London: W. Reeves.

Mauss, Marcel, 1954, *The Gift.* London: Cohen and West.

McLennan, John F., 1865, *Primitive Marriage.* Edinburgh: Adam and Charles Black.

———, 1976, *Studies in Ancient History.* London: Macmillan.

Mead, Margaret, 1928, *Coming of Age in Samoa.* New York: Morrow.

————, 1930, *Growing Up in New Guinea.* New York: Morrow.

————, 1935, *Sex and Temperament in Three Primitive Societies.* New York: Morrow.

Mead, Margaret, and Rhoda Metraux, eds., 1953, *The Study of Culture at a Distance.* Chicago: University of Chicago Press.

Merton, Robert, 1958, *Social Theory and Social Structure.* Glencoe: The Free Press.

Morgan, Lewis Henry, 1871, *Systems of Consanguinity and Affinity of the Human Family.* Washington: Smithsonian Institution.

————, 1962, *League of the Ho-de-no-sau-nee or Iroquois.* New York: Corinth Books.

————, 1963, *Ancient Society.* New York: World Publishing.

Murdock, George P., 1949, *Social Organization.* New York: Macmillan.

————, 1951, "British social anthropology." *American Anthropologist,* 53:465–73.

————, 1957, "World ethnographic sample." *American Anthropologist,* 59:664–87.

————, 1963, *Outline of World Cultures.* New Haven: Human Relations Area File Press.

Opler, Morris, 1945, "Themes as dynamic forces in culture." *American Journal of Sociology,* 51:198–206.

————, 1959, "Component, assemblage, and theme in cultural integration and differentiation." *American Anthropologist,* 61:955–64.

Perry, William J., 1923, *The Children of the Sun.* London: Methuen and Company.

Radcliffe-Brown, Alfred R., 1952, *Structure and Function in Primitive Society.* New York: The Free Press.

————, 1967, *The Andaman Islanders.* New York: The Free Press.

Rappaport, Roy A., 1968, *Pigs for the Ancestors.* New Haven: Yale University Press.

Redfield, Robert, 1930, *Tepoztlan, a Mexican Village.* Chicago: University of Chicago Press.

————, 1941, *Folk Cultures of the Yucatan.* Chicago: University of Chicago Press.

————, 1953, *The Primitive World and its Transformations.* Ithaca: Cornell University Press.

————, 1955, *The Little Community.* Chicago: University of Chicago Press.

————, 1956, *Peasant Society and Culture.* Chicago: University of Chicago Press.

Redfield, Robert, Ralph Linton, and Melville Herskovits, 1936, "Memorandum for the study of acculturation." *American Anthropologist,* 38:149–152.

Rivers, William H. R., 1900, "A genealogical method of collecting social and vital statistics." *Journal of the Royal Anthropological Institute of Great Britain and Ireland,* 30:74–82.

————, 1906, *The Todas.* New York: Macmillan.

————, 1914, *The History of Melanesian Society.* Cambridge: Cambridge University Press.

————, 1922, *History and Ethnology.* New York: Macmillan.

Rohaim, Geza, 1943, "The origin and function of culture." New York: *Nervous and Mental Disease Monographs.*

————, 1950, *Psychoanalysis and Anthropology.* New York: International University Press.

Sahlins, Marshall, and Elman Service, eds., 1960, *Evolution and Culture.* Ann Arbor: University of Michigan Press.

Sapir, Edward, 1917, "Do we need a superorganic?" *American Anthropologist,* 1917:441–47.

————, 1921, *Language.* New York: Harcourt.

————, 1924, "Culture, genuine and spurious." *Journal of Sociology,* 29:401–29.

Schaller, George, 1964, *The Year of the Gorilla.* Chicago: University of Chicago Press.

Schmidt, Wilhelm, 1939, *The Culture Historical Method of Ethnology.* New York: Fortuny's.

Schneider, David, 1968, *American Kinship.* Englewood Cliffs, N.J.: Prentice-Hall.

Schoolcraft, Henry R., 1851, *Personal Memoirs of a Residence of Thirty Years with the Indian Tribes.* Philadelphia: Lippincott.

————, 1851–1857, *Historical and Statistical Information Respecting the History, Condition, and Prospects of the Indian Tribes of the United States.* Philadelphia: Lippincott.

Smith, Grafton Elliot, 1911, *The Ancient Egyptians and their Influence upon Civilizations in Europe.* London: Harper & Row.

Spencer, Herbert, 1852, "A theory of population deduced from the general law of animal fertility." *Westminster Review,* 57:468–501.

————, 1857, "Progress: Its laws and causes." *Westminster Review,* 67:445–85.

————, 1862, "Synthetic philosophy: First principles." New York: DeWitt Revolving Fund.

————, 1876–1896, *The Principles of Sociology.* New York: D. Appleton.

Steward, Julian H., 1946–1950, "Handbook of the South American Indians." Washington: *Bureau of American Ethnology Bulletin* 143. 6 vols.

————, 1955, *Theory of Culture Change.* Urbana: University of Illinois Press.

Tönnies, Ferdinand, 1967, *Community and Society.* New York: Harper Torchbooks.

Turner, Victor, 1967, *The Forest of Symbols.* Ithaca: Cornell University Press.

Tylor, Edward Burnett, 1879, "On the game of patolli in ancient America and its probable Asiatic origin." *Journal of the Royal Anthropological Institute of Great Britain and Ireland,* 8:116–29.

————, 1958, *Primitive Culture.* (2 vols.) New York: Harper Torchbooks.

————, 1964, In Paul Bohannan, ed., *Researches into the Early History of Mankind and the Development of Civilization.* Chicago: University of Chicago Press.

van Gennep, Arnold, 1960, *The Rites of Passage.* Chicago: University of Chicago Press.

van Lawick-Goodall, Jane, 1971, *In the Shadow of Man.* New York: Houghton Mifflin.

Vayda, Andrew P., ed., 1969, *Environment and Cultural Behavior.* Garden City, N.Y.: Natural History Press.

Wallace, Anthony F. C., 1970, *Culture and Personality.* New York: Random House.

White, Leslie, 1949, *The Science of Culture.* New York: Grove Press.

————, 1959, *The Evolution of Culture.* New York: McGraw-Hill.

Whiting, John, and Irvin Child, 1953, *Child Training and Personality: A Cross-Cultural Study.* New Haven: Yale University Press.

Wissler, Clark, 1917, *The American Indian.* New York: McMurtrie.

————, 1923, *Man and Culture.* New York: Crowell.

————, 1926, *The Relation of Nature to Man in Aboriginal America.* New York: Oxford University Press.

Index